DISCIPLE *of* CHRIST

EDUCATION IN VIRTUE®

THE PASCHAL *Mystery*
OF CHRIST

LENTEN JOURNAL

Published by Lumen Ecclesiae Press
4101 East Joy Road
Ann Arbor, Michigan 48105

Editor: Sister John Dominic Rasmussen, O.P.
Contributors: Dominican Sisters of Mary, Mother of the Eucharist
Cover Design: Amy Beers
Book Design Layout and Permissions: Linda Kelly
Copy Editor: Claudia Volkman

ISBN 978-0-9982607-9-2

First Printing
Printed in the United States of America

TABLE OF CONTENTS

St. John, the beloved apostle, was an eye witness to Christ's public life, from the moment he first left his father on the shore to the moment Jesus was taken up to heaven. John provides a testimony of what it means to be an eye witness to Jesus Christ.

"What was from the beginning, what we have heard, what we have seen with our eyes, what we looked upon and touched with our hands concerns the Word of life— for the life was made visible; we have seen it and testify to it and proclaim to you the eternal life that was with the Father and was made visible to us—what we have seen and heard we proclaim now to you, so that you too may have fellowship with us; for our fellowship is with the Father and with his Son, Jesus Christ. We are writing this so that our joy may be complete"
(1 JOHN 1:1–4).

Jesus Christ is alive! He is "the same yesterday, today, and forever" (Hebrews 13:8). To be a disciple of Christ means to know Him personally and bear witness to Him. Just as the apostles and disciples spent time with Jesus, you too are called to do likewise.

The season of Lent is the time to renew your desire to be a disciple of Christ. The three forms of penance—fasting, praying, almsgiving—are a means for you to hear, look upon, and touch Him. Therefore, I invite you to take a few moments to prayerfully examine your personal relationship with Him. For guidance let us return to John's letter:

"We have heard him." ...***HAVE YOU HEARD JESUS?***

"We have seen with our eyes." ...***HAVE YOU LOOKED UPON HIM?***

"We have touched with our hands." ...***HAVE YOU TOUCHED HIM?***

FASTING

HAVE YOU HEARD HIM?

To hear and experience the presence of God requires silence and a willingness to listen. Fasting is a means to strike an interior balance and to refrain from overindulging in any activity. It assists in decreasing the noise and busyness which prevent you from hearing Him.

HAVE YOU LOOKED UPON HIM?

Prayer is a relationship, a conversation, a personal encounter with God—in sum, talking to God from one's heart. A story told by St. John Vianney describes how you can look upon Christ. He noticed an older gentleman regularly sitting in church and asked him what he did for those long periods of time. The man answered, "I look at him and he looks at me."

PRAYER

ALMSGIVING

HAVE YOU TOUCHED HIM?

"Amen I say to you, whatever you did for one of the least brothers of mine, you did for me" (Matthew 25:40). In Jesus' teaching about the judgment on all nations (Matthew 25:31–46), He says that when you reach out and give of yourself to others, you touch Him. This gift of self enables you to find yourself and cleanse your heart of selfishness and greed (Luke 11:41).

Jesus Christ is alive! He is looking at you with love because He first loved you (John 4:19). He is inviting you to be an eye witness. Don't be afraid to spend the next forty days reading and meditating on the Word of God, for "indeed, the word of God is living and effective, sharper than any two-edged sword" (Hebrews 4:12).

Ask yourself the following question: Have I heard Him, seen Him, touched Him? In doing so you can respond to His call "those who wish to be my disciples must take up their cross and follow me" (Matthew 16:24).

Turn to pages 106–112 to prepare for Lent.

How to Use This Journal

THE SEASON OF LENT IS A TIME OF EMBRACING PENANCE TO DRAW NEAR TO CHRIST. THE VARIOUS PARTS OF THIS JOURNAL ARE INTENDED TO HELP YOU LOVE JESUS MORE AND LIVE AS A DISCIPLE OF CHRIST.

PREPARATION FOR LENT (PP. 106–112): The preparation for Lent section is intended to help you prepare for a fruitful Lent. Spend time reading the section and decide upon a "Plan for Lent" for yourself. Pray to the Holy Spirit to assist you in your personal preparation. (A teacher may wish to guide the students through the preparation.)

LECTIO DIVINA: Read the Gospel passage for each day of Lent. The questions are written to guide your prayerful reading of the Scripture.

GRATITUDE LOG: The gratitude log is included with each daily Scripture passage.

RELIGIOUS ARTWORK: The paintings have been selected to assist you in your meditations. Spend time prayerfully studying the images. You may wish to research the artist and the time period of the painting.

VISUAL JOURNEY OF CHRIST'S PASSION: Good Friday includes a visual journey of Christ's passion. This is an expansion of the Stations of the Cross. Let the beauty of these paintings enrich your meditation on the Passion.

The Lenten season can seem somber as you focus on living penance from the heart and practicing its forms. It is important to keep your heart centered on Easter and God's love for you. It can be easy to fall into a spirit of negativity and only see your mistakes. Therefore, it is essential to keep in mind God's goodness and love.

Make an effort each day to write about something that made you happy and give praise to God.

Psalm 150

Hallelujah!

Praise God in his holy sanctuary;
give praise in the mighty dome
of heaven.

Give praise for his mighty deeds,
praise him for his great majesty.

Give praise with blasts upon the horn,
praise him with harp and lyre.

Give praise with tambourines and dance
praise him with strings and pipes.

Give praise with crashing cymbals,
praise him with sounding cymbals.

Let everything that has breath
give praise to the LORD!

Hallelujah!

LECTIO DIVINA

Living Lent with the Word

As you open your mind and heart to the Holy Spirit and encounter the Word of God, you will begin to experience a renewed faith and a closer relationship with the person of Jesus Christ. The questions are written to guide your prayerful reading of Scripture and assist you in understanding the passage. They are not intended to be questions to complete for an assignment but more of a means for you to establish a relationship with Jesus.

In a spirit of recollection, place yourself in God's presence.

Recite the Prayer:

Praise Lord Jesus Christ, Son of the Living God,
Have mercy on me, a sinner.

Daily Read the Scripture Verses:

Follow the steps for *lectio divina*. Let the Word of God penetrate your mind and heart and throughout the course of the day ponder the Word.

Reading *(Lectio)*
What does the Word of God say?
Read slowly, listening attentively to the Word of God.

Meditation *(meditatio)*
What does the Word of God say to me?
Spend time with the word or phrase that touched your heart.

Prayer *(oratio)*
What do I say to the Lord in response to His Word?
Let the word or phrase shape your response to God, such as praise, petition, thanksgiving.

Contemplation *(contemplatio)*
What conversion of mind, heart, and life is the Lord asking of me?
Rest in His presence, and open your heart to receive His Love.

Action *(actio)*
How has encountering God's love in His Word changed me? How can my life be a gift to others?
Ask the Lord to show you where to grow in virtue.

> *"Let us be silent in order to hear the Lord's word and to meditate upon it, so that by the working of the Holy Spirit it may remain in our hearts and speak to us all the days of our lives."* —*Pope Benedict XVI*

MEDITATION

Mary "kept all these things, pondering them in her heart" (Luke 2:19; cf. 2:51b).

"...day after day, in the silence of ordinary life, Mary continued to treasure in her heart the sequence of marvelous events that she witnessed until the supreme test of the Cross and and the glory of the Resurrection."

PRAYER

"Mary, precisely because of her interior attitude of listening, is capable of interpreting her own history, recognizing with humility that it is the Lord who is acting. In visiting her cousin Elizabeth, she breaks into a prayer of praise and joy, the celebration of divine grace, which has filled her heart and her life, making her the Mother of the Lord."

CONTEMPLATION

"Mary, was a peerless model of contemplation of Christ. The face of the Son belonged to her in a special way because he had been knit together in her womb and had taken a human likeness from her. No one has contemplated Jesus as diligently as Mary. The gaze of her heart was already focused on him at the moment of the Annunciation, when she conceived him through the action of the Holy Spirit."

ACTION

"The last mention of Mary in the two writings of Saint Luke takes place on Saturday: the day of God's rest after the Creation, the day of silence after the death of Jesus, and the day of waiting for his Resurrection. And the tradition of commemorating the Holy Virgin on Saturday is rooted in this episode. Between the Ascension of the Risen One and the first Christian Pentecost, the Apostles and the Church gather with Mary to await with her the gift of the Holy Spirit, without which one cannot become a witness. She who has already received it in order to bring forth the incarnate Word shares with the whole Church the anticipation of this same gift so that in the heart of each believer, "Christ [may] be formed" (cf. Gal 4:19).

**All excerpts taken from *A School of Prayer* by Pope Benedict XVI.

Matthew 6:1-6, 16-18

Jesus said to his disciples: "Take care not to perform righteous deeds in order that people may see them; otherwise, you will have recompense from your heavenly Father. When you give alms, do not blow a trumpet before you, as the hypocrites do in the synagogues and in the streets to win the praise of others. Amen, I say to you, they have received their reward. But when you give alms, do not let your left hand know what your right is doing, so that your almsgiving may be secret. And your Father who sees in secret will repay you.

"When you pray, do not be like the hypocrites, who love to stand and pray in the synagogues and on street corners so that others may see them. Amen, I say to you, they have received their reward. But when you pray, go to your inner room, close the door, and pray to your Father in secret. And your Father who sees in secret will repay you.

"When you fast, do not look gloomy like the hypocrites. They neglect their appearance, so that they may appear to others to be fasting. Amen, I say to you, they have received their reward. But when you fast, anoint your head and wash your face, so that you may not appear to be fasting, except to your Father who is hidden. And your Father who sees what is hidden will repay you."

God's Word strikes the heart. What word or phrase touched your heart?

_____

_____

What does Jesus teach about:

Giving alms: _____

Praying: _____

Fasting: _____

"Jesus, You taught us that our Father sees the heart. Show me where I can 'blow the trumpet,' so others may see me looking gloomy." Write down ways you need to change.

_____

_____

_____

 With gratitude I praise You, God, for:

_____

_____

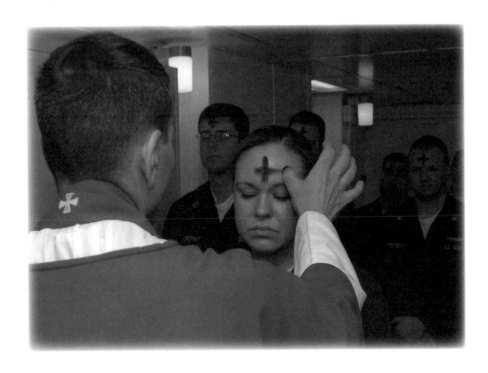

Luke 9:22-25

Jesus said to his disciples: "The Son of Man must suffer greatly and be rejected by the elders, the chief priests, and the scribes, and be killed and on the third day be raised."

Then he said to all, "If anyone wishes to come after me, he must deny himself and take up his cross daily and follow me. For whoever wishes to save his life will lose it, but whoever loses his life for my sake will save it. What profit is there for one to gain the whole world yet lose or forfeit himself?"

God's Word strikes the heart. What word or phrase touched your heart?

_____

_____

Jesus warns His disciples about His future suffering. How would this knowledge give them hope when the Son of Man suffers greatly?

_____

_____

Hope enables one to desire God above all things and to trust Him for our salvation. Jesus tells us to follow Him means to carry the cross daily. How does the theological virtue of hope strengthen us to endure our daily crosses?

_____

_____

It is hard to deny ourselves. Ask Jesus this question in prayer: "In what ways can I better carry my crosses? How can I die to self in order to bear the cross?" Write down what He says to you.

_____

_____

_____

 With gratitude I praise You, God, for:

_____

Matthew 9:14-15

The disciples of John approached Jesus and said, "Why do we and the Pharisees fast much, but your disciples do not fast?" Jesus answered them, "Can the wedding guests mourn as long as the bridegroom is with them? The days will come when the bridegroom is taken away from them, and then they will fast."

God's Word strikes the heart. What word or phrase touched your heart?

_____

_____

What is the purpose of fasting (see pages 5 and 106)?

_____

_____

Ask Jesus this question in prayer: "Jesus, show me an area in my life where Your presence is needed. How can fasting prepare me to hear You speak to me?" Write down what He says to you.

_____

_____

_____

_____

With gratitude I praise You, God, for:

_____

_____

Luke 5:27-32

Jesus saw a tax collector named Levi sitting at the customs post. He said to him, "Follow me." And leaving everything behind, he got up and followed him. Then Levi gave a great banquet for him in his house, and a large crowd of tax collectors and others were at table with them. The Pharisees and their scribes complained to his disciples, saying, "Why do you eat and drink with tax collectors and sinners?" Jesus said to them in reply, "Those who are healthy do not need a physician, but the sick do. I have not come to call the righteous to repentance but sinners."

God's Word strikes the heart. What word or phrase touched your heart?

_____

_____

What is unusual about Jesus calling Matthew (Levi) to follow Him?

_____

_____

Jesus entered the house of Matthew and ate with his friends—other tax collectors. How did the Pharisees react?

_____

_____

_____

Ask this question in prayer: "Jesus, do I judge others by their external actions? How are You showing me to not judge others?" Write down what He says to you.

_____

_____

_____

With gratitude I praise You, God, for:

_____

TRY NOT TO JUDGE PEOPLE. IF YOU JUDGE OTHERS THEN YOU ARE NOT GIVING LOVE. INSTEAD, TRY TO HELP THEM BY SEEING THEIR NEEDS AND ACTING TO MEET THEM. IT ISN'T WHAT ANYONE MAY OR MAY NOT HAVE DONE, BUT WHAT YOU HAVE DONE THAT MATTERS IN GOD'S EYES.

— BLESSED MOTHER TERESA OF CALCUTTA

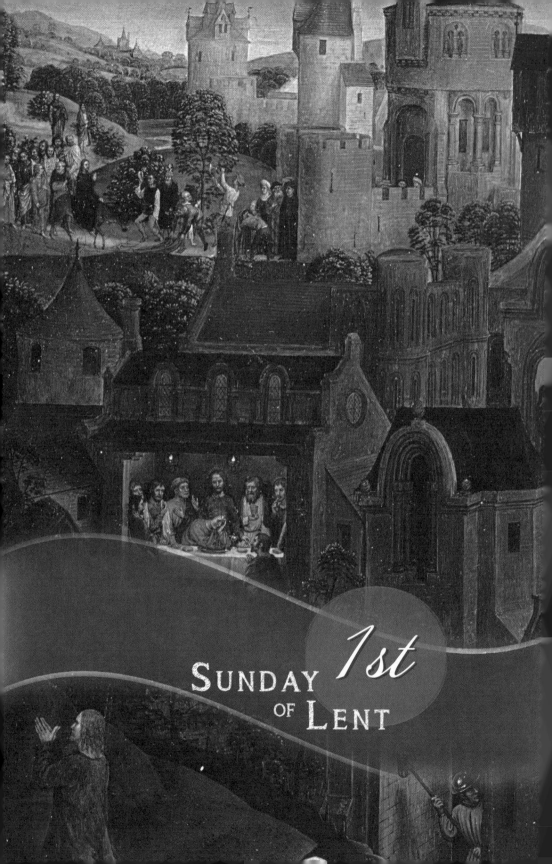

SUNDAY 1st OF LENT

YEAR A	2021, 2022, 2024	MATTHEW 4:1-11
YEAR B	2018, 2022, 2025	MARK 1:12-15
YEAR C	2019, 2023, 2026	LUKE 4:12-13

Jesus, may I listen as You speak to me.

Reading *(Lectio)*
What does the Word of God say?

Meditation *(meditatio)*
What does the Word of God say to me?

Prayer *(oratio)*
What do I say to the Lord in response to His Word?

Contemplation *(contemplatio)*
What conversion of mind, heart, and life is the Lord asking of me?

Action *(actio)*
How has encountering God's love in His Word changed me? How can my life be a gift to others?

Reflect upon the Mass readings or homily. What is a word or phrase you will carry within your heart throughout the week?

_____

_____

_____

Select one verse from the reading and memorize it.

Matthew 25:31-46

Jesus said to his disciples: "When the Son of Man comes in his glory, and all the angels with him, he will sit upon his glorious throne, and all the nations will be assembled before him. And he will separate them one from another, as a shepherd separates the sheep from the goats. He will place the sheep on his right and the goats on his left. Then the king will say to those on his right, 'Come, you who are blessed by my Father. Inherit the kingdom prepared for you from the foundation of the world. For I was hungry and you gave me food, I was thirsty and you gave me drink, a stranger and you welcomed me, naked and you clothed me, ill and you cared for me, in prison and you visited me.' Then the righteous will answer him and say, 'Lord, when did we see you hungry and feed you, or thirsty and give you drink? When did we see you a stranger and welcome you, or naked and clothe you? When did we see you ill or in prison, and visit you?' And the king will say to them in reply, 'Amen, I say to you, whatever you did for one of these least brothers of mine, you did for me.' Then he will say to those on his left, 'Depart from me, you accursed, into the eternal fire prepared for the Devil and his angels. For I was hungry and you gave me no food, I was thirsty and you gave me no drink, a stranger and you gave me no welcome, naked and you gave me no clothing, ill and in prison, and you did not care for me.' Then they will answer and say, 'Lord, when did we see you hungry or thirsty or a stranger or naked or ill or in prison, and not minister to your needs?' He will answer them, 'Amen, I say to you, what you did not do for one of these least ones, you did not do for me.' And these will go off to eternal punishment, but the righteous to eternal life."

God's Word strikes the heart. What word or phrase touched your heart?

_____

_____

What acts of mercy did the sheep perform?

_____

_____

_____

Describe the sins of the goats.

_____

_____

_____

Examine your own life. How do you:

Give to the hungry? _____

_____

Give drink to the thirsty? _____

_____

Welcome a stranger? _____

_____

Clothe those in need? _____

_____

Care for the sick? _____

_____

Visit those imprisoned? _____

_____

Ask this question in prayer: "Jesus, it is easy to become selfish and think only of my wants. Help me to be more generous toward the least ones. Show me one way I can change." Write down what He says to you.

_____

_____

_____

With gratitude I praise You, God, for:

_____

_____

Matthew 6:7-15

Jesus said to his disciples: "In praying, do not babble like the pagans, who think that they will be heard because of their many words. Do not be like them. Your Father knows what you need before you ask him.

"This is how you are to pray:

Our Father who art in heaven,
    hallowed be thy name,
thy Kingdom come
    thy will be done,
on earth as it is in heaven.
    Give us this day our daily bread
and forgive us our trespasses,
    as we forgive those who trespass against us;
and lead us not into temptation,
    but deliver us from evil.

"If you forgive men their transgressions, your heavenly Father will forgive you. But if you do not forgive men, neither will your Father forgive your transgressions."

God's Word strikes the heart. What word or phrase touched your heart?

_____

_____

What is your favorite line of the Our Father? Why?

_____

_____

_____

_____

"Jesus, my merciful Savior, give me grace to forgive those who transgress against me for to nurse a grudge keeps me from living freely." Ask Jesus to free your heart from a grudge. Write down what He says to you.

_____

_____

_____

_____

 With gratitude I praise You, God, for:

_____

_____

LENTEN
CHECKPOINT

To forgive is difficult if the other person has not expressed remorse or an apology. Ask yourself if you have failed to humbly apologize to someone. If so, pray for that person and find an occasion to express your apology.

Luke 11:29-32

While still more people gathered in the crowd, Jesus said to them, "This generation is an evil generation; it seeks a sign, but no sign will be given it, except the sign of Jonah. Just as Jonah became a sign to the Ninevites, so will the Son of Man be to this generation. At the judgment the queen of the south will rise with the men of this generation and she will condemn them, because she came from the ends of the earth to hear the wisdom of Solomon, and there is something greater than Solomon here. At the judgment the men of Nineveh will arise with this generation and condemn it, because at the preaching of Jonah they repented, and there is something greater than Jonah here."

God's Word strikes the heart. What word or phrase touched your heart?

_____

_____

Recall the Old Testament story of Jonah and how he led the Ninevites to prayer and penance. Jesus is the Son of Man. How is He a sign to this generation?

_____

_____

What virtues are necessary for a person to be able to hear teachings and preaching about Jesus (see pages 131–132)?

_____

_____

Ask the Holy Spirit, who is the Spirit of Truth, to open your heart so you may hear God's Word. Write down one distraction you experience in prayer.

_____

_____

With gratitude I praise You, God, for:

_____

_____

Matthew 7:7-12

Jesus said to his disciples: "Ask and it will be given to you; seek and you will find; knock and the door will be opened to you. For everyone who asks, receives; and the one who seeks, finds; and to the one who knocks, the door will be opened. Which one of you would hand his son a stone when he asked for a loaf of bread, or a snake when he asked for a fish? If you then, who are wicked, know how to give good gifts to your children, how much more will your heavenly Father give good things to those who ask him.

"Do to others whatever you would have them do to you. This is the law and the prophets."

God's Word strikes the heart. What word or phrase touched your heart?

_____

_____

John was present when Jesus taught the disciples about prayers of petition. He would later write, "Beloved: we have this confidence in him that if we ask anything according to his will, he hears us" (1 John 5:14). What does this teach you about prayer?

_____

_____

Ask this question in prayer: "Jesus, You lived each moment in obedience to Your heavenly Father's will. How can I learn to trust Him and believe He will not give me a stone instead of bread?" Listen in silence and write about a time He answered your prayers.

_____

_____

_____

_____

 With gratitude I praise You, God, for:

_____

_____

Matthew 5:20-26

Jesus said to his disciples: "I tell you, unless your righteousness surpasses that of the scribes and Pharisees, you will not enter into the Kingdom of heaven.

"You have heard that it was said to your ancestors, You shall not kill; and whoever kills will be liable to judgment. But I say to you, whoever is angry with his brother will be liable to judgment, and whoever says to his brother, *Raqa*, will be answerable to the Sanhedrin, and whoever says, 'You fool,' will be liable to fiery Gehenna. Therefore, if you bring your gift to the altar, and there recall that your brother has anything against you, leave your gift there at the altar, go first and be reconciled with your brother, and then come and offer your gift. Settle with your opponent quickly while on the way to court. Otherwise your opponent will hand you over to the judge, and the judge will hand you over to the guard, and you will be thrown into prison. Amen, I say to you, you will not be released until you have paid the last penny."

God's Word strikes the heart. What word or phrase touched your heart?

_____

_____

Justice enables one to give to each, beginning with God, what is due to him. How does Jesus challenge His disciples to live justly?

_____

_____

What virtues are necessary for one to live righteously? Describe how this is different than the scribes and Pharisees.

_____

_____

_____

Sometimes people are unwilling to accept our apology or forgiveness. Ask Jesus to teach you how to reconcile with those who refuse to be reconciled. Write a prayer which reflects His message to you.

_____

_____

_____

ON MAY 13, 1981 MEHMET ALI AGCA (LEFT) OPENED FIRE ON POPE SAINT JOHN PAUL II DURING A WEDNESDAY AUDIENCE IN ST. PETER'S SQUARE. POPE JOHN PAUL II SURVIVED THE FOUR GUNSHOT WOUNDS AND AGCA WAS IMMEDIATELY APPREHENDED BY THE ITALIAN POLICE. WISHING TO SHARE WITH THE WORLD AN IMAGE OF FORGIVENESS, JOHN PAUL II INVITED A PHOTOGRAPHER AND CAMERAMAN WHEN HE VISITED AGCA'S PRISON CELL IN 1983. FOR OVER 20 MINUTES THE TWO SAT, KNEE TO KNEE, IN THE FARTHEST CORNER OF THE CELL, OUT OF EARSHOT FROM THE SPECTATORS.

 With gratitude I praise You, God, for:

_____

_____

Matthew 5:43-48

Jesus said to his disciples: "You have heard that it was said, You shall love your neighbor and hate your enemy. But I say to you, love your enemies, and pray for those who persecute you, that you may be children of your heavenly Father, for he makes his sun rise on the bad and the good, and causes rain to fall on the just and the unjust. For if you love those who love you, what recompense will you have? Do not the tax collectors do the same? And if you greet your brothers and sisters only, what is unusual about that? Do not the pagans do the same? So be perfect, just as your heavenly Father is perfect."

God's Word strikes the heart. What word or phrase touched your heart?

_____

_____

Jesus shows you how to be a child of His Father. What are you called to do?

_____

_____

Jesus says, "So be perfect, just as your heavenly Father is perfect." This statement can seem almost impossible. What are some characteristics of God the Father you can imitate?

_____

_____

"Jesus, it is hard to love those who are unkind and in particular those who intentionally speak ill of me. Enlighten my mind to recognize how I treat other people and give me the grace to pray for them." Write down what Jesus reveals to you.

_____

_____

_____

"LOVE YOUR ENEMIES AND PRAY FOR THOSE WHO PERSECUTE YOU, SO THAT YOU MAY BE CHILDREN OF YOUR FATHER WHO IS IN HEAVEN; FOR HE MAKES HIS SUN RISE ON THE EVIL AND THE GOOD AND SENDS RAIN ON THE JUST AND THE UNJUST" (MT 5:44—45)! TO LOVE THOSE WHO HAVE OFFENDED US IS TO DISARM THEM AND TO TURN EVEN A BATTLEF IELDINTO AN ARENA OF MUTUAL SUPPORT AND COOPERATION.

CHRISTIANS MUST MAKE PEACE EVEN WHEN THEY FEEL THAT THEY ARE VICTIMS OF THOSE WHO HAVE STRUCK AND HURT THEM UNJUSTLY. THIS WAS HOW THE LORD HIMSELF ACTED. HE EXPECTS HIS DISCIPLE TO FOLLOW HIM, AND IN THIS WAY COOPERATE IN REDEEMING HIS BROTHERS AND SISTERS.

MAY THIS TIME OF PENANCE AND RECONCILIATION ENCOURAGE BELIEVERS TO THINK AND ACT ACCORDING TO TRUE CHARITY, OPEN TO EVERY HUMAN CIRCUMSTANCE.

— MESSAGE FOR LENT 2001
POPE SAINT JOHN PAUL II

 With gratitude I praise You, God, for:

_____

_____

SUNDAY 2nd
OF LENT

Sunday Reading

YEAR A	2021, 2022, 2024	MATTHEW 17:1–9
YEAR B	2018, 2022, 2025	MARK 9:2–10
YEAR C	2019, 2023, 2026	LUKE 9:28b–36

Jesus, may I listen as You speak to me.

Reading *(Lectio)*
What does the Word of God say?

Meditation *(meditatio)*
What does the Word of God say to me?

Prayer *(oratio)*
What do I say to the Lord in response to His Word?

Contemplation *(contemplatio)*
What conversion of mind, heart, and life is the Lord asking of me?

Action *(actio)*
How has encountering God's love in His Word changed me? How can my life be a gift to others?

Reflect upon the Mass readings or homily. What is a word or phrase you will carry within your heart throughout the week?

_____

_____

_____

Select one verse from the reading and memorize it.

MONDAY OF THE SECOND WEEK OF LENT

 Luke 6:36-38

Jesus said to his disciples: "Be merciful, just as your Father is merciful.

"Stop judging and you will not be judged. Stop condemning and you will not be condemned. Forgive and you will be forgiven. Give and gifts will be given to you; a good measure, packed together, shaken down, and overflowing, will be poured into your lap. For the measure with which you measure will in return be measured out to you."

God's Word strikes the heart. What word or phrase touched your heart?

_____

_____

Think of a time you have been judged by another person. Were you hurt or upset? Why or why not?

_____

_____

Think of a time you have judged or condemned others. How did you feel?

_____

_____

"Jesus, You revealed to us the merciful heart of Your heavenly Father. Show me when I am quick to judge others so I may change." Write down what He says to you.

_____

_____

_____

With gratitude I praise You, God, for:

_____

_____

TUESDAY OF THE SECOND WEEK OF LENT

 Matthew 23:1-12

Jesus spoke to the crowds and to his disciples, saying, "The scribes and the Pharisees have taken their seat on the chair of Moses. Therefore, do and observe all things whatsoever they tell you, but do not follow their example. For they preach but they do not practice. They tie up heavy burdens hard to carry and lay them on people's shoulders, but they will not lift a finger to move them. All their works are performed to be seen. They widen their phylacteries and lengthen their tassels. They love places of honor at banquets, seats of honor in synagogues, greetings in marketplaces, and the salutation 'Rabbi.' As for you, do not be called 'Rabbi.' You have but one teacher, and you are all brothers. Call no one on earth your father; you have but one Father in heaven. Do not be called 'Master'; you have but one master, the Christ. The greatest among you must be your servant. Whoever exalts himself will be humbled; but whoever humbles himself will be exalted."

God's Word strikes the heart. What word or phrase touched your heart?

_____

_____

How do you feel when someone says one thing but does the opposite?

_____

_____

Jesus boldly speaks about the hypocrisy of scribes and Pharisees. How is humility the solution to "exalting ourselves"? What other virtues should you seek to practice (see pages 131–132)?

_____

_____

Ask this question in prayer: "Jesus, meek and humble of heart, how do I exalt myself or fail to live what I preach to others?" Write down what He says to you.

_____

_____

With gratitude I praise You, God, for:

_____

Matthew 20:17-28

As Jesus was going up to Jerusalem, he took the Twelve disciples aside by themselves, and said to them on the way, "Behold, we are going up to Jerusalem, and the Son of Man will be handed over to the chief priests and the scribes, and they will condemn him to death, and hand him over to the Gentiles to be mocked and scourged and crucified, and he will be raised on the third day."

Then the mother of the sons of Zebedee approached Jesus with her sons and did him homage, wishing to ask him for something. He said to her, "What do you wish?" She answered him, "Command that these two sons of mine sit, one at your right and the other at your left, in your kingdom." Jesus said in reply, "You do not know what you are asking. Can you drink the chalice that I am going to drink?" They said to him, "We can." He replied, "My chalice you will indeed drink, but to sit at my right and at my left, this is not mine to give but is for those for whom it has been prepared by my Father." When the ten heard this, they became indignant at the two brothers. But Jesus summoned them and said, "You know that the rulers of the Gentiles lord it over them, and the great ones make their authority over them felt. But it shall not be so among you. Rather, whoever wishes to be great among you shall be your servant; whoever wishes to be first among you shall be your slave. Just so, the Son of Man did not come to be served but to serve and to give his life as a ransom for many."

God's Word strikes the heart. What word or phrase touched your heart?

_____

_____

How do you think the disciples felt when Jesus predicted His death and resurrection?

_____

_____

When Jesus replied to the mother of the sons of Zebedee, "You do not know what you are asking," what do you think He meant?

_____

_____

_____

Jesus said, "The Son of Man did not come to be served but to serve and to give his life as a ransom for many." How did Jesus serve and give His life as a ransom?

_____

_____

_____

Ask this question in prayer: "Jesus, at times it is hard to serve others. How can I better serve others?" Write down what He says to you.

_____

_____

_____

With gratitude I praise You, God, for:

_____

_____

LENTEN CHECKPOINT

Out of love, Jesus took His disciples aside and told them about His future suffering, crucifixion, and resurrection. During Lent our penance helps us to prepare for the times we are asked to join with Christ and carry our cross. Spend a few moments reflecting upon your Lenten journey and write your thoughts.

_____

_____

_____

Luke 16:19-31

Jesus said to the Pharisees: "There was a rich man who dressed in purple garments and fine linen and dined sumptuously each day. And lying at his door was a poor man named Lazarus, covered with sores, who would gladly have eaten his fill of the scraps that fell from the rich man's table. Dogs even used to come and lick his sores. When the poor man died, he was carried away by angels to the bosom of Abraham. The rich man also died and was buried, and from the netherworld, where he was in torment, he raised his eyes and saw Abraham far off and Lazarus at his side. And he cried out, 'Father Abraham, have pity on me. Send Lazarus to dip the tip of his finger in water and cool my tongue, for I am suffering torment in these flames.' Abraham replied, 'My child, remember that you received what was good during your lifetime while Lazarus likewise received what was bad; but now he is comforted here, whereas you are tormented. Moreover, between us and you a great chasm is established to prevent anyone from crossing who might wish to go from our side to yours or from your side to ours.' He said, 'Then I beg you, father, send him to my father's house, for I have five brothers, so that he may warn them, lest they too come to this place of torment.' But Abraham replied, 'They have Moses and the prophets. Let them listen to them.' He said, 'Oh no, father Abraham, but if someone from the dead goes to them, they will repent.' Then Abraham said, 'If they will not listen to Moses and the prophets, neither will they be persuaded if someone should rise from the dead.'"

God's Word strikes the heart. What word or phrase touched your heart?

_____

_____

Compare the rich man and Lazarus before and after their deaths.

	Rich Man	Lazarus
Before Death		
After Death		

What is the great divide?

_____

_____

_____

_____

_____

The five brothers were unable to listen to the teachings of Moses and the prophets. The sins of lust and gluttony cause spiritual blindness and a lack of desire to love God. How can fasting help you to see God and believe?

_____

_____

_____

Jesus, You taught us, "Blessed are the poor in spirit, for theirs is the kingdom of heaven" (Matthew 5:2). Ask Jesus this question in prayer: "In what ways do I treasure the things of this world as opposed to laying up treasures in heaven?" (see Matthew 6:19–21). Write down what He says to you.

_____

_____

_____

 With gratitude I praise You, God, for:

_____

_____

Matthew 21:33-43, 45-46

Jesus said to the chief priests and the elders of the people: "Hear another parable. There was a landowner who planted a vineyard, put a hedge around it, dug a wine press in it, and built a tower. Then he leased it to tenants and went on a journey. When vintage time drew near, he sent his servants to the tenants to obtain his produce. But the tenants seized the servants and one they beat, another they killed, and a third they stoned. Again he sent other servants, more numerous than the first ones, but they treated them in the same way. Finally, he sent his son to them, thinking, 'They will respect my son.' But when the tenants saw the son, they said to one another, 'This is the heir. Come, let us kill him and acquire his inheritance.' They seized him, threw him out of the vineyard, and killed him. What will the owner of the vineyard do to those tenants when he comes?" They answered him, "He will put those wretched men to a wretched death and lease his vineyard to other tenants who will give him the produce at the proper times." Jesus said to them, "Did you never read in the Scriptures:

The stone that the builders rejected
*   has become the cornerstone;*
by the Lord has this been done,
*   and it is wonderful in our eyes?*

Therefore, I say to you, the Kingdom of God will be taken away from you and given to a people that will produce its fruit." When the chief priests and the Pharisees heard his parables, they knew that he was speaking about them. And although they were attempting to arrest him, they feared the crowds, for they regarded him as a prophet.

God's Word strikes the heart. What word or phrase touched your heart?

_____

_____

"…who will give him the produce at the proper time." What do you think this means? How can you produce good works at the proper time?

_____

_____

Jesus, You are the stone rejected by the builders, and yet You became the cornerstone. Show me the ways I reject You as the cornerstone of my soul. What must I do to place my hope and trust in You? (Write down what He says to you.)

_____

_____

_____

"CHRIST ALONE IS THE
CORNERSTONE ON WHICH
IT IS POSSIBLE SOLIDLY TO
BUILD ONE'S EXISTENCE.
ONLY CHRIST—KNOWN,
CONTEMPLATED AND LOVED—
IS THE FAITHFUL FRIEND WHO
NEVER LETS US DOWN, WHO
BECOMES OUR TRAVELLING
COMPANION, AND WHOSE
WORDS WARM OUR HEARTS."
(SEE LK 24:13—35)

— WORLD YOUTH DAY 2002
POPE ST. JOHN PAUL II

 With gratitude I praise You, God, for:

_____

_____

Luke 15:1-3, 11-32

Tax collectors and sinners were all drawing near to listen to Jesus, but the Pharisees and scribes began to complain, saying, "This man welcomes sinners and eats with them."

So to them Jesus addressed this parable. "A man had two sons, and the younger son said to his father, 'Father, give me the share of your estate that should come to me.' So the father divided the property between them.

After a few days, the younger son collected all his belongings and set off to a distant country where he squandered his inheritance on a life of dissipation. When he had freely spent everything, a severe famine struck that country, and he found himself in dire need. So he hired himself out to one of the local citizens who sent him to his farm to tend the swine. And he longed to eat his fill of the pods on which the swine fed, but nobody gave him any.

Coming to his senses he thought, 'How many of my father's hired workers have more than enough food to eat, but here am I, dying from hunger. I shall get up and go to my father and I shall say to him, "Father, I have sinned against heaven and against you. I no longer deserve to be called your son; treat me as you would treat one of your hired workers."'

So he got up and went back to his father. While he was still a long way off, his father caught sight of him, and was filled with compassion. He ran to his son, embraced him and kissed him. His son said to him, 'Father, I have sinned against heaven and against you; I no longer deserve to be called your son.'

But his father ordered his servants, 'Quickly, bring the finest robe and put it on him; put a ring on his finger and sandals on his feet. Take the fattened calf and slaughter it. Then let us celebrate with a feast, because this son of mine was dead, and has come to life again; he was lost, and has been found.' Then the celebration began.

Now the older son had been out in the field and, on his way back, as he neared the house, he heard the sound of music and dancing. He called one of the servants and asked what this might mean. The servant said to him, 'Your brother has returned and your father has slaughtered the fattened calf because he has him back safe and sound.' He became angry, and when he refused to enter the house, his father came out and pleaded with him. He said to his father in reply, 'Look, all these years I served you and not once did I disobey your orders; yet you never gave me even a young goat to feast on with my friends. But when your son returns who swallowed up your property with prostitutes, for him you slaughter the fattened calf.'

He said to him, 'My son, you are here with me always; everything I have is yours. But now we must celebrate and rejoice, because your brother was dead and has come to life again; he was lost and has been found."

God's Word strikes the heart. What word or phrase touched your heart?

_____

_____

The father, who ran to his son and embraced and kissed him, represents God the Father who first loved us and seeks us. How will this knowledge sustain you in difficult situations?

_____

_____

_____

_____

_____

_____

_____

_____

If you are afraid to confess a sin, how does this parable give you the courage to take a step toward conversion and repentance? Write a prayer asking the Holy Spirit to convict you of God's merciful love.

_____

_____

_____

_____

With gratitude I praise You, God, for:

_____

_____

SUNDAY 3rd of LENT

 Sunday Reading

YEAR A	2021, 2022, 2024	JOHN 4:5-42 (OR 4:5-15, 19B-26, 39, 34-38)
YEAR B	2018, 2022, 2025	JOHN 2:13-25
YEAR C	2019, 2023, 2026	LUKE 13:1-9

Jesus, may I listen as You speak to me.

Reading *(Lectio)*
  What does the Word of God say?

Meditation *(meditatio)*
  What does the Word of God say to me?

Prayer *(oratio)*
  What do I say to the Lord in response to His Word?

Contemplation *(contemplatio)*
  What conversion of mind, heart, and life is the Lord asking of me?

Action *(actio)*
  How has encountering God's love in His Word changed me? How can my life be a gift to others?

Reflect upon the Mass readings or homily. What is a word or phrase you will carry within your heart throughout the week?

_____

_____

_____

Select one verse from the reading and memorize it.

Luke 4:24-30

Jesus said to the people in the synagogue at Nazareth: "Amen, I say to you, no prophet is accepted in his own native place. Indeed, I tell you, there were many widows in Israel in the days of Elijah when the sky was closed for three and a half years and a severe famine spread over the entire land. It was to none of these that Elijah was sent, but only to a widow in Zarephath in the land of Sidon. Again, there were many lepers in Israel during the time of Elisha the prophet; yet not one of them was cleansed, but only Naaman the Syrian." When the people in the synagogue heard this, they were all filled with fury. They rose up, drove him out of the town, and led him to the brow of the hill on which their town had been built, to hurl him down headlong. But he passed through the midst of them and went away.

God's Word strikes the heart. What word or phrase touched your heart?

_____

_____

Jesus returns to His home town of Nazareth after traveling in the region of Capernaum. He enters the synagogue and reads from the scroll of the prophet Isaiah. How is this passage fulfilled in Jesus?

_____

_____

Why did the people of Nazareth reject Jesus' teaching? How did they react? How is their response different from those in Capernaum (see Mark 1:21–22)?

_____

_____

_____

_____

Ask Jesus this question in prayer: "Is there an area in my life where I am blind or held captive? Show me how I need to change." Write down what He says to you.

_____

_____

_____

_____

_____

 With gratitude I praise you, God, for:

_____

_____

Matthew 18:21-35

Peter approached Jesus and asked him, "Lord, if my brother sins against me, how often must I forgive him? As many as seven times?" Jesus answered, "I say to you, not seven times but seventy–seven times. That is why the Kingdom of heaven may be likened to a king who decided to settle accounts with his servants. When he began the accounting, a debtor was brought before him who owed him a huge amount. Since he had no way of paying it back, his master ordered him to be sold, along with his wife, his children, and all his property, in payment of the debt. At that, the servant fell down, did him homage, and said, 'Be patient with me, and I will pay you back in full.' Moved with compassion the master of that servant let him go and forgave him the loan. When that servant had left, he found one of his fellow servants who owed him a much smaller amount. He seized him and started to choke him, demanding, 'Pay back what you owe.' Falling to his knees, his fellow servant begged him, 'Be patient with me, and I will pay you back.' But he refused. Instead, he had him put in prison until he paid back the debt. Now when his fellow servants saw what had happened, they were deeply disturbed, and went to their master and reported the whole affair. His master summoned him and said to him, 'You wicked servant! I forgave you your entire debt because you begged me to. Should you not have had pity on your fellow servant, as I had pity on you?' Then in anger his master handed him over to the torturers until he should pay back the whole debt. So will my heavenly Father do to you, unless each of you forgives your brother from your heart."

God's Word strikes the heart. What word or phrase touched your heart?

_____

_____

Justice enables one, beginning with God, to give to each what is due him. How did the servant act unjustly? In order for his entire debt to be forgiven, what must happen?

_____

_____

_____

Ask this question in prayer: "Jesus, You reveal to us the justice and mercy of Your heavenly Father, who forgives us seventy–seven times. Who have I failed to forgive? In what ways is my heart judgmental?" Write down what He says to you.

_____

_____

_____

LENTEN
CHECKPOINT

Look at your plan for Lent (p. 112). How would you describe your faithfulness to each form of penance?

Fasting: _____
_____

Prayer: _____
_____

Almsgiving: _____
_____

Since the beginning of Lent, you may have experienced unplanned sacrifices. How well have you said yes? Write down your thoughts.

_____
_____
_____
_____

 With gratitude I praise you, God, for:

_____
_____

Matthew 5:17-19

Jesus said to his disciples: "Do not think that I have come to abolish the law or the prophets. I have come not to abolish but to fulfill. Amen, I say to you, until heaven and earth pass away, not the smallest letter or the smallest part of a letter will pass from the law, until all things have taken place. Therefore, whoever breaks one of the least of these commandments and teaches others to do so will be called least in the Kingdom of heaven. But whoever obeys and teaches these commandments will be called greatest in the Kingdom of heaven."

God's Word strikes the heart. What word or phrase touched your heart?

_____

_____

Jesus teaches the importance of obeying and teaching the commandments. Why is it important to both obey and teach the commandments?

_____

_____

_____

Ask this question in prayer: "Jesus, to be Your disciple means to obey and teach all the commandments. How have I failed to obey even the smallest part in loving God and neighbor?" Write down what He says to you.

_____

_____

_____

_____

With gratitude I praise You, God, for:

_____

_____

 Luke 11:14-23

Jesus was driving out a demon that was mute, and when the demon had gone out, the mute man spoke and the crowds were amazed. Some of them said, "By the power of Beelzebul, the prince of demons, he drives out demons." Others, to test him, asked him for a sign from heaven. But he knew their thoughts and said to them, "Every kingdom divided against itself will be laid waste and house will fall against house. And if Satan is divided against himself, how will his kingdom stand? For you say that it is by Beelzebul that I drive out demons. If I, then, drive out demons by Beelzebul, by whom do your own people drive them out? Therefore they will be your judges. But if it is by the finger of God that I drive out demons, then the Kingdom of God has come upon you. When a strong man fully armed guards his palace, his possessions are safe. But when one stronger than he attacks and overcomes him, he takes away the armor on which he relied and distributes the spoils. Whoever is not with me is against me, and whoever does not gather with me scatters."

God's Word strikes the heart. What word or phrase touched your heart?

_____

_____

What do you think Jesus meant by saying, "Every kingdom divided against itself will be laid waste and will fall against house"?

_____

_____

Why can Jesus drive out demons "by the finger of God"?

_____

_____

_____

Ask this question in prayer: "Jesus, most powerful, show me which virtues I need to cultivate to maintain an armor for protection against the devil." Write down what He says to you.

_____

_____

_____

_____

 With gratitude I praise you, God, for:

_____

_____

RECITE THE "ST. MICHAEL PRAYER

ST. MICHAEL, THE ARCHANGEL, DEFEND US IN BATTLE. BE OUR PROTECTION AGAINST THE WICKEDNESS AND SNARES OF THE DEVIL. MAY GOD REBUKE HIM, WE HUMBLY PRAY, AND DO THOU, O PRINCE OF THE HEAVENLY HOSTS, BY THE POWER OF GOD, CAST INTO HELL SATAN AND ALL THE EVIL SPIRITS WHO PROWL THROUGHOUT THE WORLD SEEKING THE RUIN OF SOULS.

Friday of the Third Week of Lent

 Mark 12:28b-34

One of the scribes came to Jesus and asked him, "Which is the first of all the commandments?" Jesus replied, "The first is this: Hear, O Israel! The Lord our God is Lord alone! You shall love the Lord your God with all your heart, with all your soul, with all your mind, and with all your strength. The second is this: You shall love your neighbor as yourself. There is no other commandment greater than these." The scribe said to him, "Well said, teacher. You are right in saying, He is One and there is no other than he. And to love him with all your heart, with all your understanding, with all your strength, and to love your neighbor as yourself is worth more than all burnt offerings and sacrifices." And when Jesus saw that he answered with understanding, he said to him, "You are not far from the Kingdom of God." And no one dared to ask him any more questions.

God's Word strikes the heart. What word or phrase touched your heart?

_____

_____

Jesus acknowledges that the scribe's answer shows his understanding. Why is love of God and neighbor worth more than any burnt offering and sacrifice?

_____

_____

_____

"You shall love your neighbor as yourself." What does this mean? How can you practically live this teaching of Jesus?

_____

_____

_____

"Jesus, King of Kings, You said to the scribe, 'You are not far from the Kingdom of God.' What would You say to me?" Write down what He says to you.

_____

_____

_____

_____

 With gratitude I praise You, God, for:

_____

_____

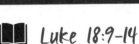 **Luke 18:9-14**

Jesus addressed this parable to those who were convinced of their own righteousness and despised everyone else. "Two people went up to the temple area to pray; one was a Pharisee and the other was a tax collector. The Pharisee took up his position and spoke this prayer to himself, 'O God, I thank you that I am not like the rest of humanity—greedy, dishonest, adulterous—or even like this tax collector. I fast twice a week, and I pay tithes on my whole income.' but the tax collector stood off at a distance and would not even raise his eyes to heaven but beat his breast and prayed, 'O God, be merciful to me a sinner.' I tell you, the latter went home justified, not the former; for everyone who exalts himself will be humbled, and the one who humbles himself will be exalted."

God's Word strikes the heart. What word or phrase touched your heart?

_____

_____

Describe the two people in the parable:

Pharisee: _____

_____

Tax Collector: _____

_____

The Pharisee believed that his "burnt offering and sacrifices" made him righteous in God's eyes. What sins do you think prevented him from loving God and neighbor?

_____

Ask this question in prayer: "Jesus, merciful and just, it is easy to judge others. Show me how I need to be more merciful." Write down what He says to you.

_____

_____

With gratitude I praise You, God, for:

_____

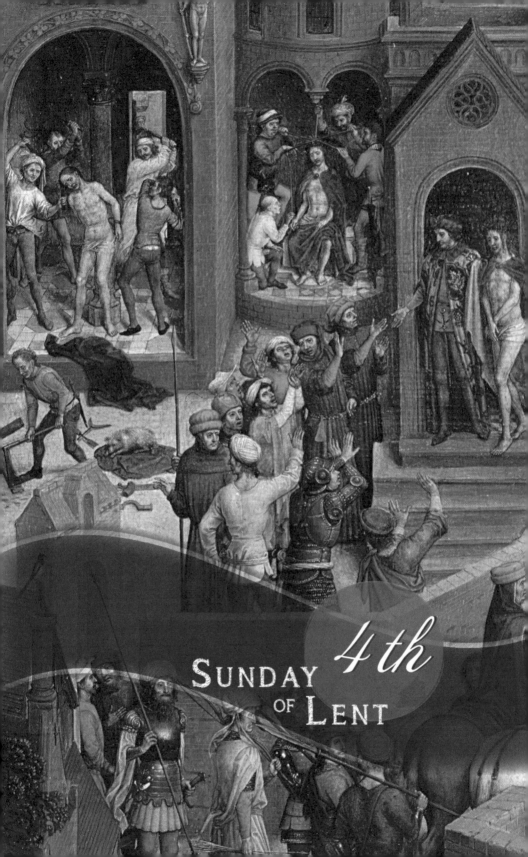

SUNDAY *4th* OF LENT

 **Sunday Reading**

YEAR A	2021, 2022, 2024	JOHN 9:1–41 (OR 9:1, 6–9, 13–17, 34–38)
YEAR B	2018, 2022, 2025	JOHN 3:14–21
YEAR C	2019, 2023, 2026	LUKE 15:1–3, 11–32

Jesus, may I listen as You speak to me.

Reading *(Lectio)*
What does the Word of God say?

Meditation *(meditatio)*
What does the Word of God say to me?

Prayer *(oratio)*
What do I say to the Lord in response to His Word?

Contemplation *(contemplatio)*
What conversion of mind, heart, and life is the Lord asking of me?

Action *(actio)*
How has encountering God's love in His Word changed me? How can my life be a gift to others?

Reflect upon the Mass readings or homily. What is a word or phrase you will carry within your heart throughout the week?

_____

_____

_____

Select one verse from the reading and memorize it.

John 4:43-54

At that time Jesus left [Samaria] for Galilee. For Jesus himself testified that a prophet has no honor in his native place. When he came into Galilee, the Galileans welcomed him, since they had seen all he had done in Jerusalem at the feast; for they themselves had gone to the feast.

Then he returned to Cana in Galilee, where he had made the water wine. Now there was a royal official whose son was ill in Capernaum. When he heard that Jesus had arrived in Galilee from Judea, he went to him and asked him to come down and heal his son, who was near death. Jesus said to him, "Unless you people see signs and wonders, you will not believe." The royal official said to him, "Sir, come down before my child dies." Jesus said to him, "You may go; your son will live." The man believed what Jesus said to him and left. While the man was on his way back, his slaves met him and told him that his boy would live. He asked them when he began to recover. They told him, "The fever left him yesterday, about one in the afternoon." The father realized that just at that time Jesus had said to him, "Your son will live," and he and his whole household came to believe. Now this was the second sign Jesus did when he came to Galilee from Judea.

God's Word strikes the heart. What word or phrase touched your heart?

_____

_____

An act of faith requires one to believe and trust in God without "signs and wonders." How does the royal official practice an act of faith when Jesus says, "You may go; your son will live"?

_____

When the royal official encountered Jesus, he believed His words, "You may go; your son will live." What happened to his family?

_____

Jesus, it is easier to believe when I see "signs and wonders." How does my faith need to increase so I may believe like the royal official? (Write down what you hear Him say.)

_____

_____

_____

_____

 With gratitude I praise You, God, for:

_____

_____

John 5:1-3a; 5-16

There was a feast of the Jews, and Jesus went up to Jerusalem. Now there is in Jerusalem at the Sheep Gate a pool called in Hebrew Bethesda, with five porticoes. In these lay a large number of ill, blind, lame, and crippled. One man was there who had been ill for thirty-eight years. When Jesus saw him lying there and knew that he had been ill for a long time, he said to him, "Do you want to be well?" The sick man answered him, "Sir, I have no one to put me into the pool when the water is stirred up; while I am on my way, someone else gets down there before me." Jesus said to him, "Rise, take up your mat, and walk." Immediately the man became well, took up his mat, and walked.

Now that day was a sabbath. So the Jews said to the man who was cured, "It is the sabbath, and it is not lawful for you to carry your mat." He answered them, "The man who made me well told me, 'Take up your mat and walk.'" They asked him, "Who is the man who told you, 'Take it up and walk'?" The man who was healed did not know who it was, for Jesus had slipped away, since there was a crowd there. After this Jesus found him in the temple area and said to him, "Look, you are well; do not sin any more, so that nothing worse may happen to you." The man went and told the Jews that Jesus was the one who had made him well. Therefore, the Jews began to persecute Jesus because he did this on a sabbath.

God's Word strikes the heart. What word or phrase touched your heart?

_____

_____

Jesus' grandparents, Ann and Joachim, lived in Jerusalem near the Sheep Gate. Do you think Jesus had seen that man before?

_____

Jesus asked the man, "Do you want to be well?" What did Jesus tell him to do?

_____

After his healing, Jesus sees him again. What does He say to him?

_____

_____

The man is healed once he picks up his mat. Ask Jesus these questions in prayer: "How can I be healed by willingly accepting my illness or suffering? Is there something in my life which is preventing me from freely walking as a disciple of Christ?" Write down what He says to you.

_____

_____

_____

_____

LENTEN CHECKPOINT

Life is filled with many distractions which prevent us from listening to Jesus. He may be asking you, "Do you want to be well?" For the next week try to unplug for a period of time from a device.

 With gratitude I praise You, God, for:

_____

_____

John 5:17-30

Jesus answered the Jews: "My Father is at work until now, so I am at work." For this reason they tried all the more to kill him, because he not only broke the sabbath but he also called God his own father, making himself equal to God.

Jesus answered and said to them, "Amen, amen, I say to you, the Son cannot do anything on his own, but only what he sees the Father doing; for what he does, the Son will do also. For the Father loves the Son and shows him everything that he himself does, and he will show him greater works than these, so that you may be amazed. For just as the Father raises the dead and gives life, so also does the Son give life to whomever he wishes. Nor does the Father judge anyone, but he has given all judgment to the Son, so that all may honor the Son just as they honor the Father. Whoever does not honor the Son does not honor the Father who sent him. Amen, amen, I say to you, whoever hears my word and believes in the one who sent me has eternal life and will not come to condemnation, but has passed from death to life. Amen, amen, I say to you, the hour is coming and is now here when the dead will hear the voice of the Son of God, and those who hear will live. For just as the Father has life in himself, so also he gave to the Son the possession of life in himself. And he gave him power to exercise judgment, because he is the Son of Man. Do not be amazed at this, because the hour is coming in which all who are in the tombs will hear his voice and will come out, those who have done good deeds to the resurrection of life, but those who have done wicked deeds to the resurrection of condemnation.

"I cannot do anything on my own; I judge as I hear, and my judgment is just, because I do not seek my own will but the will of the one who sent me."

God's Word strikes the heart. What word or phrase touched your heart?

_____

_____

Jesus' words deeply disturbed the Jews, and they wanted to kill Him. Despite their anger, Jesus answered them. What does His teaching reveal to us about God the Father?

_____

_____

With gratitude I praise You, God, for:

_____

 John 5:31-47

Jesus said to the Jews: "If I testify on my own behalf, my testimony is not true. But there is another who testifies on my behalf, and I know that the testimony he gives on my behalf is true. You sent emissaries to John, and he testified to the truth. I do not accept human testimony, but I say this so that you may be saved. He was a burning and shining lamp, and for a while you were content to rejoice in his light. But I have testimony greater than John's. The works that the Father gave me to accomplish, these works that I perform testify on my behalf that the Father has sent me. Moreover, the Father who sent me has testified on my behalf. But you have never heard his voice nor seen his form, and you do not have his word remaining in you, because you do not believe in the one whom he has sent. You search the Scriptures, because you think you have eternal life through them; even they testify on my behalf. But you do not want to come to me to have life.

"I do not accept human praise; moreover, I know that you do not have the love of God in you. I came in the name of my Father, but you do not accept me; yet if another comes in his own name, you will accept him. How can you believe, when you accept praise from one another and do not seek the praise that comes from the only God? Do not think that I will accuse you before the Father: the one who will accuse you is Moses, in whom you have placed your hope. For if you had believed Moses, you would have believed me, because he wrote about me. But if you do not believe his writings, how will you believe my words?"

God's Word strikes the heart. What word or phrase touched your heart?

_____

_____

Jesus is trying to reason with the Jews, but they will not open their minds and hearts. He says, "But you do not want to come to me to have life." Does this same stubbornness exist in our age? What does it look and sound like?

_____

_____

_____

_____

Ask this question in prayer: "Jesus, show me how I may be stubborn like the Jews and fail to come to You." Write down what He says to you.

_____

_____

_____

_____

 With gratitude I praise You, God, for:

_____

_____

RECITE THE FOLLOWING ASPIRATIONS

LORD, I DO BELIEVE, HELP MY UNBELIEF.

SACRED HEART OF JESUS, I TRUST IN YOU.

JESUS GENTLE AND HUMBLE OF HEART.

MAKE MY HEART LIKE UNTO THINE.

BLESSED IS HE WHO COMES IN THE NAME OF THE LORD.

John 7:1-2, 10, 25-30

Jesus moved about within Galilee; he did not wish to travel in Judea, because the Jews were trying to kill him. But the Jewish feast of Tabernacles was near.

But when his brothers had gone up to the feast, he himself also went up, not openly but as it were in secret.

Some of the inhabitants of Jerusalem said, "Is he not the one they are trying to kill? And look, he is speaking openly and they say nothing to him. Could the authorities have realized that he is the Christ? But we know where he is from. When the Christ comes, no one will know where he is from." So Jesus cried out in the temple area as he was teaching and said, "You know me and also know where I am from. Yet I did not come on my own, but the one who sent me, whom you do not know, is true. I know him, because I am from him, and he sent me." So they tried to arrest him, but no one laid a hand upon him, because his hour had not yet come.

God's Word strikes the heart. What word or phrase touched your heart?

_____

_____

Jesus continues to preach to those in Galilee. Yet when He traveled in Judea, He was rejected by the Jews. Why do you think John described in detail how Jesus cried out in the temple area?

_____

_____

Ask this question in prayer: "Jesus, despite the rejection of the Jews, You continued to teach and proclaim the truth. It can be hard and discouraging to speak and have other people reject truth. How can I cultivate the virtues of fortitude and perseverance in my daily life?" Write down what He says to you.

_____

_____

_____

 With gratitude I praise You, God, for:

_____

John 7:40-53

Some in the crowd who heard these words of Jesus said, "This is truly the Prophet." Others said, "This is the Christ." But others said, "The Christ will not come from Galilee, will he? Does not Scripture say that the Christ will be of David's family and come from Bethlehem, the village where David lived?" So a division occurred in the crowd because of him. Some of them even wanted to arrest him, but no one laid hands on him.

So the guards went to the chief priests and Pharisees, who asked them, "Why did you not bring him?" The guards answered, "Never before has anyone spoken like this man." So the Pharisees answered them, "Have you also been deceived? Have any of the authorities or the Pharisees believed in him? But this crowd, which does not know the law, is accursed." Nicodemus, one of their members who had come to him earlier, said to them, "Does our law condemn a man before it first hears him and finds out what he is doing?" They answered and said to him, "You are not from Galilee also, are you? Look and see that no prophet arises from Galilee."

Then each went to his own house.

God's Word strikes the heart. What word or phrase touched your heart?

_____

_____

Describe how the different people in the crowd respond to Jesus.

_____

_____

_____

John wrote about Nicodemus' visit to Jesus at night (John 3:1–21). Why do think his reaction is different?

_____

_____

_____

_____

Ask this question in prayer: "Jesus, even today people react differently to you. Some accept you as the Christ, and many do not. Nicodemus had a docile heart and a courageous spirit. How can I live more faithfully as Your disciple?" Write down what He says to you.

_____

_____

_____

_____

 With gratitude I praise you, God, for:

_____

_____

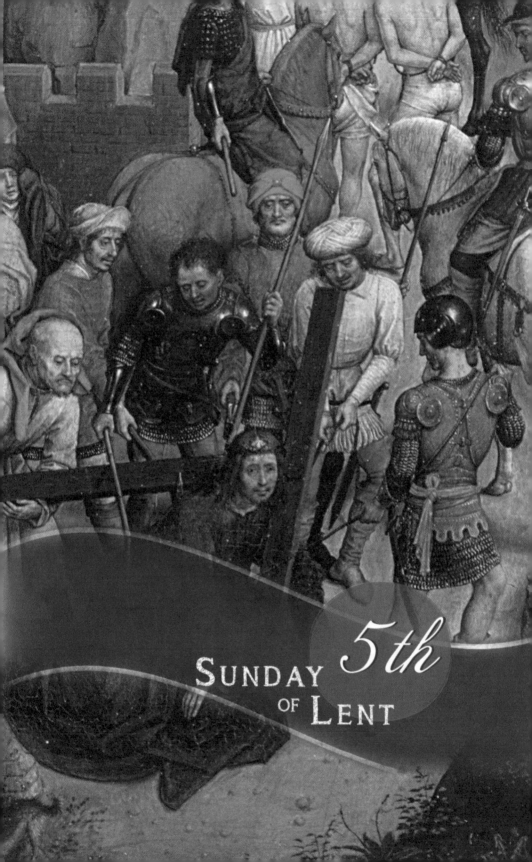

Sunday 5th
of Lent

 Sunday Reading

YEAR **A**	2021, 2022, 2024	JOHN 11:1–45 (OR 11:3-7, 17, 20-27, 33B-45)
YEAR **B**	2018, 2022, 2025	JOHN 12:20–33
YEAR **C**	2019, 2023, 2026	JOHN 8:1–11

Jesus, may I listen as You speak to me.

Reading *(Lectio)*
What does the Word of God say?

Meditation *(meditatio)*
What does the Word of God say to me?

Prayer *(oratio)*
What do I say to the Lord in response to His Word?

Contemplation *(contemplatio)*
What conversion of mind, heart, and life is the Lord asking of me?

Action *(actio)*
How has encountering God's love in His Word changed me? How can my life be a gift to others?

Reflect upon the Mass readings or homily. What is a word or phrase you will carry within your heart throughout the week?

_____

_____

_____

Select one verse from the reading and memorize it.

 *John 8:1-11*

Jesus went to the Mount of Olives. But early in the morning he arrived again in the temple area, and all the people started coming to him, and he sat down and taught them. Then the scribes and the Pharisees brought a woman who had been caught in adultery and made her stand in the middle. They said to him, "Teacher, this woman was caught in the very act of committing adultery. Now in the law, Moses commanded us to stone such women. So what do you say?" They said this to test him, so that they could have some charge to bring against him. Jesus bent down and began to write on the ground with his finger. But when they continued asking him, he straightened up and said to them, "Let the one among you who is without sin be the first to throw a stone at her." Again he bent down and wrote on the ground. And in response, they went away one by one, beginning with the elders. So he was left alone with the woman before him. Then Jesus straightened up and said to her, "Woman, where are they? Has no one condemned you?" She replied, "No one, sir." Then Jesus said, "Neither do I condemn you. Go, and from now on do not sin any more."

God's Word strikes the heart. What word or phrase touched your heart?

_____

_____

What do you think the scribes and Pharisees expected Jesus to do?

_____

_____

With His finger, Jesus writes on the ground, and everyone drops their stones and walks away. What do you think Jesus wrote?

_____

_____

_____

"Jesus, You said that by the 'finger of God' You cast out demons. Touch my heart with Your finger so that You may cast out any demons which prevent me from loving You and others. What stones of sin and judgment do I need to let go of?" Write down what He says to you.

_____

_____

_____

_____

 With gratitude I praise you, God, for:

_____

_____

John 8:21-30

Jesus said to the Pharisees: "I am going away and you will look for me, but you will die in your sin. Where I am going you cannot come." So the Jews said, "He is not going to kill himself, is he, because he said, 'Where I am going you cannot come'?" He said to them, "You belong to what is below, I belong to what is above. You belong to this world, but I do not belong to this world. That is why I told you that you will die in your sins. For if you do not believe that I AM, you will die in your sins." So they said to him, "Who are you?" Jesus said to them, "What I told you from the beginning. I have much to say about you in condemnation. But the one who sent me is true, and what I heard from him I tell the world." They did not realize that he was speaking to them of the Father. So Jesus said to them, "When you lift up the Son of Man, then you will realize that I AM, and that I do nothing on my own, but I say only what the Father taught me. The one who sent me is with me. He has not left me alone, because I always do what is pleasing to him." Because he spoke this way, many came to believe in him.

God's Word strikes the heart. What word or phrase touched your heart?

_____

_____

How does Jesus respond to the Jews' question, "Who are you?"

_____

_____

_____

Why is it essential for them and for us to believe that Jesus is "I AM?"

_____

_____

Jesus, You instruct us in the ways that You are "I AM." Reveal to me one way in which I need to ponder within my heart, "I am the Vine," "I am the Good Shepherd," "I am the Bread of Life," "I am the Light of the World," "I am the Resurrection," "I am the Way, the Truth, and the Life." (Write down what He says to you.)

_____

_____

_____

_____

 With gratitude I praise You, God, for:

_____

_____

OBEDIENCE

Assenting to rightful authority without hesitation or resistance

JESUS SAID, "I ALWAYS DO WHAT IS PLEASING TO HIM." AS A CHILD JESUS WAS OBEDIENT TO MARY AND JOSEPH (LUKE 2:51). HIS ACTIONS WERE PLEASING TO HIS FATHER. WHY IS IT IMPORTANT FOR YOU TO OBEY AND RESPECT THOSE WHO HAVE RIGHTFUL AUTHORITY? LIST THOSE PEOPLE YOU SHOULD OBEY AND RESPECT.

_____

_____

_____

_____

John 8:31-42

Jesus said to those Jews who believed in him, "If you remain in my word, you will truly be my disciples, and you will know the truth, and the truth will set you free." They answered him, "We are descendants of Abraham and have never been enslaved to anyone. How can you say, 'You will become free'?" Jesus answered them, "Amen, amen, I say to you, everyone who commits sin is a slave of sin. A slave does not remain in a household forever, but a son always remains. So if the Son frees you, then you will truly be free. I know that you are descendants of Abraham. But you are trying to kill me, because my word has no room among you. I tell you what I have seen in the Father's presence; then do what you have heard from the Father."

They answered and said to him, "Our father is Abraham." Jesus said to them, "If you were Abraham's children, you would be doing the works of Abraham. But now you are trying to kill me, a man who has told you the truth that I heard from God; Abraham did not do this. You are doing the works of your father!" So they said to him, "We were not born of fornication. We have one Father, God." Jesus said to them, "If God were your Father, you would love me, for I came from God and am here; I did not come on my own, but he sent me."

God's Word strikes the heart. What word or phrase touched your heart?

_____

_____

What do you think Jesus means by this statement, "If you remain in my word, you will truly be…free"?

_____

_____

_____

Think of a time you have not lived in truth or spoken the truth. How were you enslaved by this lie? How were you "set free?"

_____

_____

_____

"Jesus, You are the way, the truth, and the life. Show me how remaining in Your Word strengthens me as a disciple." Write down one way you can strive to remain in His Word.

_____

_____

_____

_____

 With gratitude I praise You, God, for:

_____

_____

John 8:51-59

Jesus said to the Jews: "Amen, amen, I say to you, whoever keeps my word will never see death." So the Jews said to him, "Now we are sure that you are possessed. Abraham died, as did the prophets, yet you say, 'Whoever keeps my word will never taste death.' Are you greater than our father Abraham, who died? Or the prophets, who died? Who do you make yourself out to be?" Jesus answered, "If I glorify myself, my glory is worth nothing; but it is my Father who glorifies me, of whom you say, 'He is our God.' You do not know him, but I know him. And if I should say that I do not know him, I would be like you a liar. But I do know him and I keep his word. Abraham your father rejoiced to see my day; he saw it and was glad." So the Jews said to him, "You are not yet fifty years old and you have seen Abraham?" Jesus said to them, "Amen, amen, I say to you, before Abraham came to be, I AM." So they picked up stones to throw at him; but Jesus hid and went out of the temple area.

God's Word strikes the heart. What word or phrase touched your heart?

_____

_____

Jesus reveals to us the means to obtaining eternal life: "to never see death." What does it mean to "keep my word"?

_____

_____

_____

Jesus reveals further His relationship with His Father by stating that He knows Him and keeps His word. How do the Jews respond to Him?

_____

_____

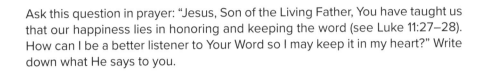

Ask this question in prayer: "Jesus, Son of the Living Father, You have taught us that our happiness lies in honoring and keeping the word (see Luke 11:27–28). How can I be a better listener to Your Word so I may keep it in my heart?" Write down what He says to you.

_____

_____

_____

_____

 With gratitude I praise You, God, for:

_____

_____

John 10:31-42

The Jews picked up rocks to stone Jesus. Jesus answered them, "I have shown you many good works from my Father. For which of these are you trying to stone me?" The Jews answered him, "We are not stoning you for a good work but for blasphemy. You, a man, are making yourself God." Jesus answered them, "Is it not written in your law, 'I said, "You are gods"'? If it calls them gods to whom the word of God came, and Scripture cannot be set aside, can you say that the one whom the Father has consecrated and sent into the world blasphemes because I said, 'I am the Son of God'? If I do not perform my Father's works, do not believe me; but if I perform them, even if you do not believe me, believe the works, so that you may realize and understand that the Father is in me and I am in the Father." Then they tried again to arrest him; but he escaped from their power.

He went back across the Jordan to the place where John first baptized, and there he remained. Many came to him and said, "John performed no sign, but everything John said about this man was true." And many there began to believe in him.

God's Word strikes the heart. What word or phrase touched your heart?

_____

_____

Jesus continues to witness by His words and deeds, but the Jews do not have "ears that hear." Why do they threaten to stone Him or have Him arrested?

_____

_____

When Jesus departed Jerusalem and crossed the Jordan river, how was He received?

_____

_____

Describe the difference between the Jews and those who came to see Jesus.

_____

_____

_____

Ask this question in prayer: "Jesus, those who were baptized by John had recognized their sins and repented. How am I in need of repentance so I may seek You more fully?" Write down what He says to you.

_____

_____

_____

 With gratitude I praise You, God, for:

_____

_____

John 11:45-56

Many of the Jews who had come to Mary and seen what Jesus had done began to believe in him. But some of them went to the Pharisees and told them what Jesus had done. So the chief priests and the Pharisees convened the Sanhedrin and said, "What are we going to do? This man is performing many signs. If we leave him alone, all will believe in him, and the Romans will come and take away both our land and our nation." But one of them, Caiaphas, who was high priest that year, said to them, "You know nothing, nor do you consider that it is better for you that one man should die instead of the people, so that the whole nation may not perish." He did not say this on his own, but since he was high priest for that year, he prophesied that Jesus was going to die for the nation, and not only for the nation, but also to gather into one the dispersed children of God. So from that day on they planned to kill him.

So Jesus no longer walked about in public among the Jews, but he left for the region near the desert, to a town called Ephraim, and there he remained with his disciples.

Now the Passover of the Jews was near, and many went up from the country to Jerusalem before Passover to purify themselves. They looked for Jesus and said to one another as they were in the temple area, "What do you think? That he will not come to the feast?"

God's Word strikes the heart. What word or phrase touched your heart?

_____

_____

The Jews went to Mary because they had witnessed Jesus raising Lazarus from the dead. Jesus' words and deeds continued to divide the Jews, so they went to the chief priests and pharisees. Describe their fears and confusion.

_____

_____

If you were a member of the Sanhedrin, how would you have responded to the question, "What are we going to do?"

_____

_____

_____

Jesus experienced rejection and knows how it feels to be hated by people. Think about a time you have felt rejected or hurt by other people. Write a short prayer to Jesus about your feelings.

_____

_____

_____

_____

LENTEN CHECKPOINT

The days of Lent prepare us to journey with Christ through His passion, death, and resurrection. If you have not faithfully lived your plan for Lent, renew your intentions and strive to be with Jesus this week. Write a prayer expressing your intentions.

_____

_____

_____

_____

 With gratitude I praise You, God, for:

_____

_____

SUNDAY *Palm*
OF THE **PASSION**
OF THE **LORD**

 **Sunday Reading**

YEAR **A**	2021, 2022, 2024	MATTHEW **26:14–42;66** (OR 27:11–54)
YEAR **B**	2018, 2022, 2025	MARK **14:1–15;47** (OR 15:1–39)
YEAR **C**	2019, 2023, 2026	LUKE **22:14–23;56** (OR 23:1–49)

Jesus, may I listen as You speak to me.

> **Reading** *(Lectio)*
> *What does the Word of God say?*
>
> **Meditation** *(meditatio)*
> *What does the Word of God say to me?*
>
> **Prayer** *(oratio)*
> *What do I say to the Lord in response to His Word?*
>
> **Contemplation** *(contemplatio)*
> *What conversion of mind, heart, and life is the Lord asking of me?*
>
> **Action** *(actio)*
> *How has encountering God's love in His Word changed me? How can my life be a gift to others?*

Reflect upon the Mass readings or homily. What is a word or phrase you will carry within your heart throughout the week?

_____

_____

_____

Select one verse from the reading and memorize it.

John 12:1-11

Six days before Passover Jesus came to Bethany, where Lazarus was, whom Jesus had raised from the dead. They gave a dinner for him there, and Martha served, while Lazarus was one of those reclining at table with him. Mary took a liter of costly perfumed oil made from genuine aromatic nard and anointed the feet of Jesus and dried them with her hair; the house was filled with the fragrance of the oil. Then Judas the Iscariot, one of his disciples, and the one who would betray him, said, "Why was this oil not sold for three hundred days' wages and given to the poor?" He said this not because he cared about the poor but because he was a thief and held the money bag and used to steal the contributions. So Jesus said, "Leave her alone. Let her keep this for the day of my burial. You always have the poor with you, but you do not always have me."

The large crowd of the Jews found out that he was there and came, not only because of him, but also to see Lazarus, whom he had raised from the dead. And the chief priests plotted to kill Lazarus too, because many of the Jews were turning away and believing in Jesus because of him.

God's Word strikes the heart. What word or phrase touched your heart?

_____

_____

Describe the action of Mary.

_____

_____

_____

Describe the action of Judas.

_____

_____

With gratitude I praise You, God, for:

_____

_____

John 13:21-33, 36-38

Reclining at table with his disciples, Jesus was deeply troubled and testified, "Amen, amen, I say to you, one of you will betray me." The disciples looked at one another, at a loss as to whom he meant. One of his disciples, the one whom Jesus loved, was reclining at Jesus' side. So Simon Peter nodded to him to find out whom he meant. He leaned back against Jesus' chest and said to him, "Master, who is it?" Jesus answered, "It is the one to whom I hand the morsel after I have dipped it." So he dipped the morsel and took it and handed it to Judas, son of Simon the Iscariot. After Judas took the morsel, Satan entered him. So Jesus said to him, "What you are going to do, do quickly." Now none of those reclining at table realized why he said this to him. Some thought that since Judas kept the money bag, Jesus had told him, "Buy what we need for the feast," or to give something to the poor. So Judas took the morsel and left at once. And it was night.

When he had left, Jesus said, "Now is the Son of Man glorified, and God is glorified in him. If God is glorified in him, God will also glorify him in himself, and he will glorify him at once. My children, I will be with you only a little while longer. You will look for me, and as I told the Jews, 'Where I go you cannot come,' so now I say it to you."

Simon Peter said to him, "Master, where are you going?" Jesus answered him, "Where I am going, you cannot follow me now, though you will follow later." Peter said to him, "Master, why can I not follow you now? I will lay down my life for you." Jesus answered, "Will you lay down your life for me? Amen, amen, I say to you, the cock will not crow before you deny me three times."

God's Word strikes the heart. What word or phrase touched your heart?

_____

_____

Can you recall other statements about the character of Judas? Write down what you remember.

_____

_____

_____

"Jesus, You loved Judas and Peter. Judas betrayed You and Peter would deny knowing You. Sadly, Judas did not believe in Your mercy and forgiveness, but Peter did." Write a prayer asking Jesus to teach you how to know and trust in His mercy.

_____

_____

_____

_____

 With gratitude I praise You, God, for:

_____

_____

Read about Peter and Judas in the following scripture sequence.

A little later the bystanders came over and said to Peter, "Surely you too are one of them; even your speech gives you away." At that he began to curse and to swear, "I do not know the man." And immediately a cock crowed. Then Peter remembered the word that Jesus had spoken: "Before the cock crows you will deny me three times." He went out and began to weep bitterly.

Peter

Matthew 14:27–33
Matthew 16:13–20
Matthew 16:21–23
Matthew 17:1–8
Matthew 26:30–35
Matthew 26:52–58
Matthew 26:69–75
John 20:1–10
John 21:1–23

Judas

John 12:4–5
Luke 22:3–4
Mark 14:10
John 13:27
John 18:5–6
Matthew 27:3–5

Then Judas, his betrayer, seeing that Jesus had been condemned, deeply regretted what he had done. He returned the thirty pieces of silver to the chief priests and elders, saying, "I have sinned in betraying innocent blood." They said, "What is that to us? Look to it yourself." Flinging the money into the temple, he departed and went off and hanged himself.

WEDNESDAY OF HOLY WEEK

 ## Matthew 26:14-25

One of the Twelve, who was called Judas Iscariot, went to the chief priests and said, "What are you willing to give me if I hand him over to you?" They paid him thirty pieces of silver, and from that time on he looked for an opportunity to hand him over.

On the first day of the Feast of Unleavened Bread, the disciples approached Jesus and said, "Where do you want us to prepare for you to eat the Passover?" He said, "Go into the city to a certain man and tell him, 'The teacher says, "My appointed time draws near; in your house I shall celebrate the Passover with my disciples."'" The disciples then did as Jesus had ordered, and prepared the Passover.

When it was evening, he reclined at table with the Twelve. And while they were eating, he said, "Amen, I say to you, one of you will betray me." Deeply distressed at this, they began to say to him one after another, "Surely it is not I, Lord?" He said in reply, "He who has dipped his hand into the dish with me is the one who will betray me. The Son of Man indeed goes, as it is written of him, but woe to that man by whom the Son of Man is betrayed. It would be better for that man if he had never been born." Then Judas, his betrayer, said in reply, "Surely it is not I, Rabbi?" He answered, "You have said so."

God's Word strikes the heart. What word or phrase touched your heart?

_____

_____

Recall how Judas had complained about the oil worth three hundred days' wages being poured out in the anointing. Now he betrays Christ for thirty pieces of silver. What does this show about Judas?

_____

_____

When Jesus describes the person who will betray him, He says, "It would be better for that man if he had never been born." What do you think this means?

_____

_____

_____

Judas states, "Jesus, surely it is not I, Rabbi?" which indicates a denial of his betrayal of the heart. "Jesus, show me how my sins have betrayed You and give me the grace of repentance." Write down what He reveals to you.

_____

_____

_____

_____

 With gratitude I praise You, God, for:

_____

_____

John 13:1-15

Before the feast of Passover, Jesus knew that his hour had come to pass from this world to the Father. He loved his own in the world and he loved them to the end. The devil had already induced Judas, son of Simon the Iscariot, to hand him over. So, during supper, fully aware that the Father had put everything into his power and that he had come from God and was returning to God, he rose from supper and took off his outer garments. He took a towel and tied it around his waist. Then he poured water into a basin and began to wash the disciples' feet and dry them with the towel around his waist. He came to Simon Peter, who said to him, "Master, are you going to wash my feet?" Jesus answered and said to him, "What I am doing, you do not understand now, but you will understand later." Peter said to him, "You will never wash my feet." Jesus answered him, "Unless I wash you, you will have no inheritance with me." Simon Peter said to him, "Master, then not only my feet, but my hands and head as well." Jesus said to him, "Whoever has bathed has no need except to have his feet washed, for he is clean all over; so you are clean, but not all." For he knew who would betray him; for this reason, he said, "Not all of you are clean."

So when he had washed their feet and put his garments back on and reclined at table again, he said to them, "Do you realize what I have done for you? You call me 'teacher' and 'master,' and rightly so, for indeed I am. If I, therefore, the master and teacher, have washed your feet, you ought to wash one another's feet. I have given you a model to follow, so that as I have done for you, you should also do."

God's Word strikes the heart. What word or phrase touched your heart?

_____

_____

Even though the devil has entered Judas' heart to betray Him, Jesus continues to teach the disciples how to live. What does the washing of the disciples' feet show about Jesus? What virtues are exemplified?

_____

_____

_____

How are you called to "wash the feet" of other people?

_____

_____

_____

Ask this question in prayer: "Jesus, meek and humble of heart, You give Yourself to us in the Eucharist. How can I draw closer to You and give of myself to others?" Write down what He says to you.

_____

_____

_____

_____

With gratitude I praise You, God, for:

_____

_____

FRIDAY OF THE PASSION OF OUR LORD (GOOD FRIDAY)

📖 John 18:1-19:42

Jesus went out with his disciples across the Kidron valley to where there was a garden, into which he and his disciples entered. Judas his betrayer also knew the place, because Jesus had often met there with his disciples. So Judas got a band of soldiers and guards from the chief priests and the Pharisees and went there with lanterns, torches, and weapons. Jesus, knowing everything that was going to happen to him, went out and said to them, "Whom are you looking for?" They answered him, "Jesus the Nazorean." He said to them, "I AM." Judas his betrayer was also with them. When he said to them, "I AM," they turned away and fell to the ground. So he again asked them, "Whom are you looking for?" They said, "Jesus the Nazorean." Jesus answered, "I told you that I AM. So if you are looking for me, let these men go." This was to fulfill what he had said, "I have not lost any of those you gave me." Then Simon Peter, who had a sword, drew it, struck the high priest's slave, and cut off his right ear. The slave's name was Malchus. Jesus said to Peter, "Put your sword into its scabbard. Shall I not drink the cup that the Father gave me?"

So the band of soldiers, the tribune, and the Jewish guards seized Jesus, bound him, and brought him to Annas first. He was the father-in-law of Caiaphas, who was high priest that year. It was Caiaphas who had counseled the Jews that it was better that one man should die rather than the people.

Simon Peter and another disciple followed Jesus. Now the other disciple was known to the high priest, and he entered the courtyard of the high priest with Jesus. But Peter stood at the gate outside. So the other disciple, the acquaintance of the high priest, went out and spoke to the gatekeeper and brought Peter in. Then the maid who was the gatekeeper said to Peter, "You are not one of this man's disciples, are you?" He said, "I am not." Now the slaves and the guards were standing around a charcoal fire that they had made, because it was cold, and were warming themselves. Peter was also standing there keeping warm.

The high priest questioned Jesus about his disciples and about his doctrine. Jesus answered him, "I have spoken publicly to the world. I have always taught in a synagogue or in the temple area where all the Jews gather, and in secret I have said nothing. Why ask me? Ask those who heard me what I said to them. They know what I said." When he had said this, one of the temple guards standing there struck Jesus and said, "Is this the way you answer the high priest?" Jesus answered him, "If I have spoken wrongly, testify to the wrong; but if I have spoken rightly, why do you strike me?" Then Annas sent him bound to Caiaphas the high priest.

Now Simon Peter was standing there keeping warm. And they said to him, "You are not one of his disciples, are you?" He denied it and said, "I am not." One of the slaves of the high priest, a relative of the one whose ear Peter had cut off, said, "Didn't I see you in the garden with him?" Again Peter denied it. And immediately the cock crowed.

When Pilate heard these words he brought Jesus out and seated him on the judge's bench in the place called Stone Pavement, in Hebrew, Gabbatha. It was preparation day for Passover, and it was about noon. And he said to the Jews, "Behold, your king!" They cried out, "Take him away, take him away! Crucify him!" Pilate said to them, "Shall I crucify your king?" The chief priests answered, "We have no king but Caesar." Then he handed him over to them to be crucified.

So they took Jesus, and, carrying the cross himself, he went out to what is called the Place of the Skull, in Hebrew, Golgotha. There they crucified him, and with him two others, one on either side, with Jesus in the middle. Pilate also had an inscription written and put on the cross. It read, "Jesus the Nazorean, the King of the Jews." Now many of the Jews read this inscription, because the place where Jesus was crucified was near the city; and it was written in Hebrew, Latin, and Greek. So the chief priests of the Jews said to Pilate, "Do not write 'The King of the Jews,' but that he said, 'I am the King of the Jews.'" Pilate answered, "What I have written, I have written."

When the soldiers had crucified Jesus, they took his clothes and divided them into four shares, a share for each soldier. They also took his tunic, but the tunic was seamless, woven in one piece from the top down. So they said to one another, "Let's not tear it, but cast lots for it to see whose it will be," in order that the passage of Scripture might be fulfilled that says:

They divided my garments among them,
     and for my vesture they cast lots.

This is what the soldiers did. Standing by the cross of Jesus were his mother and his mother's sister, Mary the wife of Clopas, and Mary of Magdala. When Jesus saw his mother and the disciple there whom he loved he said to his mother, "Woman, behold, your son." Then he said to the disciple, "Behold, your mother." And from that hour the disciple took her into his home.

After this, aware that everything was now finished, in order that the Scripture might be fulfilled, Jesus said, "I thirst." There was a vessel filled with common wine. So they put a sponge soaked in wine on a sprig of hyssop and put it up to his mouth. When Jesus had taken the wine, he said, "It is finished." And bowing his head, he handed over the spirit.

[Here all kneel and pause for a short time.]

Now since it was preparation day, in order that the bodies might not remain on the cross on the sabbath, for the sabbath day of that week was a solemn one, the Jews asked Pilate that their legs be broken and that they be taken down. So the soldiers came and broke the legs of the first and then of the other one who was crucified with Jesus. But when they came to Jesus and saw that he was already dead, they did not break his legs, but one soldier thrust his lance into his side, and immediately blood and water flowed out. An eyewitness has testified, and his testimony is true; he knows that he is speaking the truth, so that you may come to believe. For this happened so that the Scripture passage might be fulfilled: Not a bone of it will be broken. And again another passage says: They will look upon him whom they have pierced.

After this, Joseph of Arimathea, secretly a disciple of Jesus for fear of the Jews, asked Pilate if he could remove the body of Jesus. And Pilate permitted it. So he came and took his body. Nicodemus, the one who had first come to him at night, also came bringing a mixture of myrrh and aloes weighing about one hundred pounds. They took the body of Jesus and bound it with burial cloths along with the spices, according to the Jewish burial custom. Now in the place where he had been crucified there was a garden, and in the garden a new tomb, in which no one had yet been buried. So they laid Jesus there because of the Jewish preparation day; for the tomb was close by.

AFTER MEDITATING UPON THE IMAGES OF THE PASSION OF THE LORD (SEE FOLLOWING PAGES), SELECT ONE IMAGE WHICH STRUCK YOUR HEART. SPEND TIME QUIETLY LOOKING AT THE IMAGE. WRITE YOUR OWN MEDITATION.

My Meditation

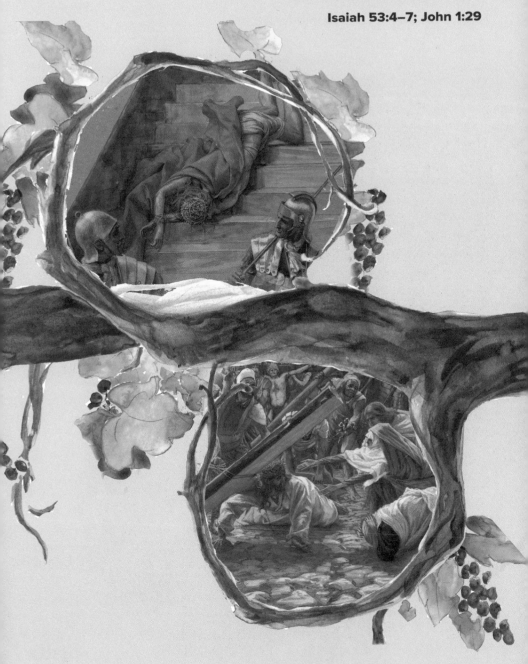

THIRD STATION:

Jesus falls for the first time

Isaiah 53:4–7; John 1:29

FOURTH STATION:

Jesus meets His mother

Lamentations 1:12; Luke 2:25–40; John 19:26–27

FIFTH STATION:

Simon of Cyrene helps Jesus carry His cross

Mark 8:34; Mark 15:21; 2 Timothy 2:3

SIXTH STATION:

Veronica wipes the face of Jesus

Isaiah 53:2–3; Matthew 25:40

Ninth Station:

Jesus falls the third time

Psalm 37:23–24; Hebrews 4:15–16

Tenth Station:

Jesus is stripped of His garments

Psalm 22:16–18; John 19:23–24

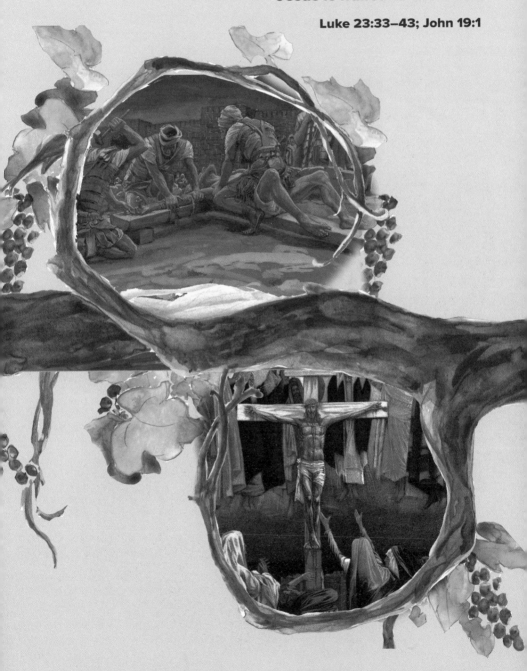

ELEVENTH STATION:

Jesus is nailed to the cross

Luke 23:33–43; John 19:1

TWELFTH STATION:

Jesus dies on the cross

Matthew 27:50; John 19:28–37

THIRTEENTH STATION:

Jesus is taken down from the cross

Psalm 22:14–15; John 19:38–40

FOURTEENTH STATION:

Jesus is laid in the tomb

Matthew 27:57–61; Mark 15:46–47

A reading from an ancient homily for Holy Saturday

What is happening? Today there is a great silence over the earth, a great silence, and stillness, a great silence because the King sleeps; the earth was in terror and was still, because God slept in the flesh and raised up those who were sleeping from the ages. God has died in the flesh, and the underworld has trembled.

Truly he goes to seek out our first parent like a lost sheep; he wishes to visit those who sit in darkness and in the shadow of death. He goes to free the prisoner Adam and his fellow–prisoner Eve from their pains, he who is God, and Adam's son.

The Lord goes in to them holding his victorious weapon, his cross. When Adam, the first created man, sees him, he strikes his breast in terror and calls out to all: "My Lord be with you all." And Christ in reply says to Adam: "And with your spirit." And grasping his hand he raises him up, saying: "Awake, O sleeper, and arise from the dead, and Christ shall give you light."

"I am your God, who for your sake became your son, who for you and your descendants now speak and command with authority those in prison: Come forth, and those in darkness: Have light, and those who sleep: Rise."

"I command you: Awake, sleeper, I have not made you to be held a prisoner in the underworld. Arise from the dead; I am the life of the dead. Arise, O man, work of my hands, arise, you who were fashioned in my image. Rise, let us go hence; for you in me and I in you, together we are one undivided person."

"For you, I your God became your son; for you, I the Master took on your form; that of slave; for you, I who am above the heavens came on earth and under the earth; for you, man, I became as a man without help, free among the dead; for you, who left a garden, I was handed over to Jews from a garden and crucified in a garden."

"Look at the spittle on my face, which I received because of you, in order to restore you to that first divine inbreathing at creation. See the blows on my cheeks, which I accepted in order to refashion your distorted form to my own image."

"See the scourging of my back, which I accepted in order to disperse the load of your sins which was laid upon your back. See my hands nailed to the tree for a good purpose, for you, who stretched out your hand to the tree for an evil one."

"I slept on the cross and a sword pierced my side, for you, who slept in paradise and brought forth Eve from your side. My side healed the pain of your side; my sleep will release you from your sleep in Hades; my sword has checked the sword which was turned against you."

"But arise, let us go hence. The enemy brought you out of the land of paradise; I will reinstate you, no longer in paradise, but on the throne of heaven. I denied you the tree of life, which was a figure, but now I myself am united to you, I who am life. I posted the cherubim to guard you as they would slaves; now I make the cherubim worship you as they would God."

"The cherubim throne has been prepared, the bearers are ready and waiting, the bridal chamber is in order, the food is provided, the everlasting houses and rooms are in readiness; the treasures of good things have been opened; the kingdom of heaven has been prepared before the ages."

📖 *John 20:1-9*

On the first day of the week, Mary of Magdala came to the tomb early in the morning, while it was still dark, and saw the stone removed from the tomb. So she ran and went to Simon Peter and to the other disciple whom Jesus loved, and told them, "They have taken the Lord from the tomb, and we don't know where they put him." So Peter and the other disciple went out and came to the tomb. They both ran, but the other disciple ran faster than Peter and arrived at the tomb first; he bent down and saw the burial cloths there, but did not go in. When Simon Peter arrived after him, he went into the tomb and saw the burial cloths there, and the cloth that had covered his head, not with the burial cloths but rolled up in a separate place. Then the other disciple also went in, the one who had arrived at the tomb first, and he saw and believed. For they did not yet understand the Scripture that he had to rise from the dead.

SOLEMNITY OF ST. JOSEPH, SPOUSE OF THE BLESSED VIRGIN MARY

📖 Matthew 1:16; 18-21; 24A

Jacob was the father of Joseph, the husband of Mary. Of her was born Jesus who is called the Christ.

Now this is how the birth of Jesus Christ came about. When his mother Mary was betrothed to Joseph, but before they lived together, she was found with child through the Holy Spirit. Joseph her husband, since he was a righteous man, yet unwilling to expose her to shame, decided to divorce her quietly. Such was his intention when, behold, the angel of the Lord appeared to him in a dream and said, "Joseph, son of David, do not be afraid to take Mary your wife into your home. For it is through the Holy Spirit that this child has been conceived in her. She will bear a son and you are to name him Jesus, because he will save his people from their sins." When Joseph awoke, he did as the angel of the Lord had commanded him and took his wife into his home.

God's Word strikes the heart. What word or phrase touched your heart?

_____

_____

Joseph had decided to divorce Mary quietly. What does this reveal about Joseph's character?

_____

_____

_____

An angel appeared to Joseph in a dream. What was his response to the message?

_____

_____

_____

St. Matthew references the words of the prophet Isaiah (Isaiah 7:14). How was this fulfilled?

_____

_____

_____

"Emmanuel" means God is with us. "Jesus, what do You want me to learn by Joseph's trust in the angel's message and Your name meaning 'God is with us?'" Write down what He says to you.

_____

_____

_____

With gratitude I praise You, God, for:

_____

_____

Solemnity of the Annunciation of the Lord

 Luke 1:26-38

The angel Gabriel was sent from God to a town of Galilee called Nazareth, to a virgin betrothed to a man named Joseph, of the house of David, and the virgin's name was Mary. And coming to her, he said, "Hail, full of grace! The Lord is with you." But she was greatly troubled at what was said and pondered what sort of greeting this might be. Then the angel said to her, "Do not be afraid, Mary, for you have found favor with God. Behold, you will conceive in your womb and bear a son, and you shall name him Jesus. He will be great and will be called Son of the Most High, and the Lord God will give him the throne of David his father, and he will rule over the house of Jacob forever, and of his Kingdom there will be no end." But Mary said to the angel, "How can this be, since I have no relations with a man?" And the angel said to her in reply, "The Holy Spirit will come upon you, and the power of the Most High will overshadow you. Therefore the child to be born will be called holy, the Son of God. And behold, Elizabeth, your relative, has also conceived a son in her old age, and this is the sixth month for her who was called barren; for nothing will be impossible for God." Mary said, "Behold, I am the handmaid of the Lord. May it be done to me according to your word." Then the angel departed from her.

God's Word strikes the heart. What word or phrase touched your heart?

_____

_____

St. Luke, a doctor, provides details about Mary and Elizabeth that emphasize the words of the angel Gabriel, "For nothing will be impossible for God." What are these details about Mary and Elizabeth? How did God intervene?

_____

_____

_____

Ask Jesus this question in prayer, "Jesus, Your mother prayerfully pondered Gabriel's message. How can I be more patient and ponder God's will for my life?" Write down what He says to you.

_____

_____

_____

 With gratitude I praise You, God, for:

_____

_____

Fasting

While fasting has traditionally been associated with refraining from food and drink, it is not limited to it. It can also include refraining from any activity you indulge in or derive pleasure from. Therefore, it is a means to strike an interior balance and master the desires of the world, pleasures of the flesh, and temptations of the devil.

Seeking to live virtuously assists the formation of good habits; that is, dispositions which enable you to properly order and harmonize your life in Christ. To determine how you can embrace fasting, quietly pause and reflect upon your daily life and patterns of behavior. The chart below and on the next two pages are intended to be general and to serve as a starting point. The questions are designed to help you reflect on where you need to limit the excess in your life in order to be freed from a sinful habit (vice).

Questions for self-reflection	Virtues to be cultivated	Ways to cultivate
• What activities consume a great deal of your time? • How long do you spend on each? • Are you able to say "no" when people pressure you to do something? • Is there anything you cannot do without? • Do you eat/drink more than you should?	TEMPERANCE (SELF-CONTROL)	Give up: • an activity which consumes your time • buying songs for your playlist or other media • a drink/food you regularly consume • snacking between meals

• How many hours do you sleep?
  Bedtime _____
  Time you rise _____
• Do you eat three healthy meals a day?
• Is your room/closet/dresser in order?
• Do you make your bed every morning?
	ORDERLINESS	• Go to bed at a reasonable time.
		• Eat three healthy meals a day.
		• Make your bed each day.
		• Clean your room/car regularly.

Questions for self-reflection	Virtues to be cultivated	Ways to cultivate
• Do you waste time doing things you shouldn't be doing? • Do you delay or "put off" doing chores or homework? • Are you easily distracted when doing tasks? Do you deliberately distract others?	INDUSTRIOUSNESS	• Make a plan for the day/week. • Place a holy card on your desk to remind you to be diligent and focused at your labors. • Do your chores first each day.
• Do you gossip or speak negatively of others? • Do you text negative messages about people? • Do you spread rumors?	JUSTICE	• Refrain from speaking ill of others. • Ask yourself if what you are going to say is true, kind, and helpful.

• What sort of casual activity do you engage in on your electronic devices?
• How much time do you spending using:
  – social media (Facebook)
  – video games, texting
  – interactive games
  – computer programs
  – listening to music
  – watching TV/movies
• Do any of these images or sounds disturb or distract you?
• Do they interfere with your ability to be pure of heart and mind?
• Does a song or image stay in your mind for a long time?
• How many songs do you have on your playlist?
• Is there a particular drink, food, or candy you enjoying having several times during the day?
• How much time do you spend working out (exercising)?
• How much of your day is given to socializing and hanging out with friends?
• Is it balanced?
	MODERATION	• Refrain from listening to your favorite songs.
		• Limit your posts or Internet time.
		• Limit use of:
		  – iPod
		  – video games
		  – consumption of energy drinks or beverages
		  – movies, TV shows

Preparation For Lent

Questions for self-reflection	Virtues to be cultivated	Ways to cultivate
• Do you have to be the center of attention? • Do you call out in class or interrupt others when they talk? • Do you try to "one-up" others?	HUMILITY	• Don't talk over others or interrupt them. • Let others be recognized. • Think before you speak. Ask yourself if it is: True, kind, and helpful. • Allow others to tell the story first.
• Do you view impure images on the Internet, TV, or in magazines? • Do you read novels that have impure content? • Do you dress in a way that reflects your dignity?	MODESTY	• Guard your eyes; don't watch shows or read materials that you know are impure. • Every time you use the computer, say a Hail Mary, Our Father, and Glory Be. • Place holy cards around your computer (remember God is there). • Say a Hail Mary every time you see something that is impure. • Ask your parents or a trust-worthy friend what they think if you are unsure if what you are wearing is modest.

Prayer

The Church says prayer is a form of penance. It is not always easy to trust God, as prayer always presupposes effort (see *CCC*, 2725–2758). We might fight against ourselves in prayer—against distractions, laziness, and temptations to stop trying. Unlike a merely human friendship, we don't always see the results of our prayers. For this reason it is tempting to give up. Pope Francis writes in his exhortation *Evangelii Gaudium* that it may be that God uses our sacrifices and prayers "to shower blessings in another part of the world which we will never visit. The Holy Spirit works as he wills, when he wills and where he wills; we entrust ourselves without pretending to see striking results. We know only that our commitment is necessary.... Let us keep marching forward; let us give him everything, allowing him to make our efforts bear fruit in his good time" (279).

Use the chart below and on the following page to help you reflect on your life of prayer.

Questions for self–reflection	Virtues to be cultivated	Ways to cultivate
• Do you make your actions a prayer? • Do you try to make your life a living prayer? • Do you thank God for His blessings?	**GRATITUDE**	• Look at the beauty of creation every day (one thing) and thank God for giving us this gift. • Thank God daily for your life and its many blessings.
• Do you pray during the time you have scheduled for prayer?	**LOYALTY**	• Make a faithful commitment to daily prayer.
• Do you "offer up" annoyances or inconveniences? • Do you pray for those who wrong you or annoy you? • Do you pray with the Scriptures? • Do you spend time in Eucharistic Adoration? • Do you pray for others? • Do you ask God to make you a better person?	**PRAYERFULNESS**	• Look for places where you can be alone with God without distractions. • Be still, offer up annoyances, pray for those who wrong you. • Pray for others and for yourself.

Preparation for Lent

Questions for self-reflection	Virtues to be cultivated	Ways to cultivate
• Do you schedule time for prayer every day?	**RESPONSIBILITY**	• Responsibly schedule a time for prayer (right before you go to bed or in the morning).
• Do you speak with Jesus from your heart?	**HONESTY**	• Share your heart with Jesus, recognizing that He "sees the heart."
• How do you spend Sundays? • How do you spend Holy Days?	**JUSTICE**	• Properly observe Sundays during Lent. • Rest, do something you enjoy doing, and pray.
• Do you pray to "just get through" your prayer time? • Do you ask God for the grace to be a better person?	**SINCERITY**	• Be sincere in your prayer.
• Do you listen and wait for God's response? • Do you seek immediate consolations in prayer? • Do you give up when God doesn't answer as you want?	**PERSEVERANCE**	• Be quiet in God's presence. • Don't give up when prayer is hard... keep trying.

God is the friend of silence. See how nature—trees, flowers, grass—grows in silence; see the stars, the moon, and the sun, how they move in silence.

—St. Teresa of Calcutta

Almsgiving

Prayerfully consider your daily life and patterns of behavior. Do you regularly give of your time and talents to others? Use the chart below to reflect on how you give alms.

Questions for self-reflection	Virtue to be cultivated	Ways to cultivate
• Do you look for opportunities to help others?	**MAGNIFICENCE**	• Give generously of your time to others. • Save some of the money you would have spent on songs, clothes, etc., and give it to the poor, your church, or a worthy organization.
• Do you do your chores or clean up without being asked? • Do you volunteer at your parish or school?	**MAGNANIMITY**	• Do more than is expected of you. • Surprise your siblings by doing their chores for them. • Volunteer at your local parish.
• Do you seek out those who are being excluded and include them?	**GENEROSITY**	• Seek out those who are being left out and invite them to hang out with you.
• How much time do you spend with others? With your siblings? • Do you intentionally exclude others?	**KINDNESS**	• Be welcoming to others. • Spend more time with your siblings. • Spend the time you would have spent on the computer helping your parents.
• Are you willing to help others? • Do you complain when you have to do work?	**COURTESY**	• Be prompt and generous when anyone asks you for your help. Better yet, do it before someone asks you.

PLAN FOR LENT

Complete the chart below to identify your "fitness plan" for Lent.

Choose a specific area for each type of penance where you want to grow in virtue. In the space provided, write down the virtue you wish to cultivate and your plan for cultivating that virtue.

Form of Penance	Virtue to Cultivate	Ways to Cultivate
Fasting		
Prayer		
Almsgiving		

Fortitude is the cardinal virtue that enables one to endure difficulties and pain for the sake of what is good. Therefore, pray for an increase of fortitude and the grace to persevere.

Prayer for Perseverance:

Below write your own prayer, asking God for the grace of perseverance in your Lenten resolutions:

_____

_____

_____

_____

_____

HOLINESS DOES NOT CONSIST
OF DOING EXTRAORDINARY
THINGS. IT CONSISTS IN
ACCEPTING, WITH A SMILE,
WHATEVER JESUS SENDS US.
IT CONSISTS IN ACCEPTING AND
FOLLOWING THE WILL OF GOD.

—ST. TERESA OF CALCUTTA

CONVERSION

The world offers you comfort. But you were not made for comfort, you were made for greatness.
—Pope Benedict XVI

pg. 116

PRAYER

Christian prayer should go further: to the knowledge of the love of the Lord Jesus, to union with him. (CCC 2708)

pg. 124

VIRTUE

Virtue is what one does passionately; Vice is what one cannot stop doing because of passion. —St. Augustine

pg. 130

GIFT OF SELF

**The worst prison would be a closed heart.
—John Paul II**

pg. 133

CONVERSION

"I AM THE VINE, YOU ARE THE BRANCHES. HE WHO ABIDES IN ME, AND I IN HIM, HE IT IS THAT BEARS MUCH FRUIT, FOR APART FROM ME YOU CAN DO NOTHING. IF A MAN DOES NOT ABIDE IN ME, HE IS CAST FORTH AS A BRANCH AND WITHERS, AND THE BRANCHES ARE GATHERED, THROWN INTO THE FIRE AND BURNED."

— John 15: 5–6

At Baptism, every Christian is immersed into the water, symbolizing burial into Christ's death and rising in Him as a 'new creature' (*CCC*, §1214).

The virtues and gifts of the Holy Spirit are infused in the life of Christians and disposes them to live in relationship with the Holy Trinity.

By recognizing your sinfulness in light of the virtues and gifts of the Holy Spirit, you are able to receive God's merciful forgiveness. The 'ways of turning away from happiness' serve as a general guideline to assist with understanding how you can sin against a virtue or gift and impede God's grace from operating within your life.

Regular confession and a willingness to change patterns of sin opens your interior life to the love of Christ, which animates the growth of the virtues and gifts and enables you to be receptive to the promptings of the Spirit. By abiding in His grace and love, you are transformed from within and freed to live in happiness, striving for Eternal Beatitude.

The practice of all the virtues is animated and inspired by charity, which 'binds everything together in perfect harmony' (Colossians 3:14, *CCC*, §1827).

DAILY EXAMINATION

As a disciple of Christ, you are called to daily conversion. That is, striving each day to live in truth and freedom. A daily examination enables you to experience God's mercy and start each day anew in Christ.

† *PRESENCE:* Place yourself in God's presence

† *PRAISE AND GRATITUDE:* Recall the blessings of the day—joys/sorrows

† *PROCESS:* Reflect upon the events of the day (your thoughts and feelings)

† *PENANCE AND CONVERSION:* Acknowledge your sins and resolve to change

† *PLAN AND PROMISE:* Intentionally plan for a new day to live receptive to God's grace

RITE OF THE SACRAMENT OF RECONCILIATION

- Greet the priest.
- Make the Sign of the Cross.
- Listen as the priest prays.
- Say, "Bless me, Father, for I have sinned. It has been (tell how long it has been) since my last confession."
- Tell your sins. You can speak about anything that is bothering you.
- Listen to the priest's advice.
- Accept your penance.
- Pray an act of contrition.
- Receive absolution, silently making the Sign of the Cross and respond saying, "Amen."
- Priest says, "Give thanks to the Lord, for He is good."
- Response: "His mercy endures forever."
- Say, "Thank You, Father."
- Make sure you do your penance.

ACT OF CONTRITION

O my God, I am heartily sorry for having offended Thee and
I detest all my sins because I dread the loss of heaven and
the pains of hell. But most of all because they have offended
Thee my God who art all good and deserving of all my love. I
firmly resolve with the help of Thy grace to confess my sins,
to do penance, and to amend my life. Amen.

CONVERSION

BELOW AND ON THE FOLLOWING PAGES, THE **'WAYS OF TURNING AWAY FROM HAPPINESS'** SERVE AS A GENERAL GUIDELINE TO ASSIST WITH UNDERSTANDING HOW ONE CAN SIN AGAINST A VIRTUE OR GIFT AND IMPEDE GOD'S GRACE FROM OPERATING WITHIN ONE'S LIFE.

SEEING WITH FAITH

FAITH: ENABLES ONE TO KNOW GOD AND ALL THAT HE HAS REVEALED

GIFT OF UNDERSTANDING: Enables one to see more deeply into the mysteries of the faith and to judge with certainty all created things

GIFT OF KNOWLEDGE: Guides one in knowing what to believe and how to share it with others

WAYS OF TURNING AWAY FROM HAPPINESS

UNBELIEF OR INFIDELITY: Have I refused to accept the truths of the faith? Have I been selective in my acceptance of Church teachings?

HERESY: Have I led others astray by teaching/condoning/promoting things contrary to Church teaching?

APOSTASY: Have I become a public scandal to my Catholic faith through bad example or public denunciation of our Church's truths?

BLASPHEMY: Have I held God in contempt through my speech (swearing), actions or thoughts? Have I held priests, religious, or anything that is sacred in contempt (i.e. the rosary, scapular, the Sacraments)?

BLINDNESS OF MIND (ARISES FROM LUST): Have I neglected my prayer/spiritual life? Are fulfilling my passions more important than attending to my spiritual life?

DULLNESS OF SENSE (ARISES FROM GLUTTONY): Have I become lazy in seeking the truths of the faith? Have I become complacent in accepting what the Church teaches?

CONVERSION

ABIDING with HOPE

HOPE: ENABLES ONE TO DESIRE GOD ABOVE ALL THINGS AND TO TRUST HIM FOR PERSONAL SALVATION

GIFT OF FEAR OF THE LORD: Brings forth the fear of offending God by sin

HUMILITY: Awareness that all one's gifts come from God and the appreciation for the gifts of others

WAYS OF TURNING AWAY FROM HAPPINESS

DESPAIR: Have I thought that God could not forgive me my sins? Has my spiritual laziness (acedia) or unchastity caused me to lose hope in God's mercy?

PRESUMPTION: Have I committed sin by presuming God's forgiveness? Have I relied solely on my own capabilities as sufficient to handle anything?

ACEDIA: Have I neglected to observe the Lord's day? Am I unable to pursue and maintain a relationship with God? Do work and other activities consume my interests?

BURNING with CHARITY

CHARITY: ENABLES ONE TO LOVE AS GOD HIMSELF LOVES; INCLUDES LOVING GOD ABOVE ALL THINGS AND ONE'S NEIGHBOR AS ONESELF

GIFT OF WISDOM: Moves one to order one's life according to God's will

KINDNESS: Expressing genuine concern about the well-being of others, anticipating the needs of others

GENEROSITY: Giving of oneself in a willing, cheerful manner for the good of others

WAYS OF TURNING AWAY FROM HAPPINESS

HATRED OF GOD: Have I hated God as a result of my own pride and envy? Have I hated God because of my distaste/disdain for the penalty of sin? Have I hated God for some evil that has befallen me?

ENVY: Have I rejoiced in someone else's misfortune? Have I been jealous of others?

DISCORD/CONTENTION: Do I vehemently argue a point even when I know I might be wrong?

FOLLY: Have I made poor decisions in regards to the good of my soul because I am too attached to material things?

 **LOVING** WITH **JUSTICE**

JUSTICE: ENABLES ONE TO GIVE TO EACH, BEGINNING WITH GOD, WHAT IS DUE HIM

GIFT OF PIETY: Inclines one as a child of God to have devotion and honor to God as Father

GRATITUDE: Thankful disposition of mind and heart

OBEDIENCE: Assenting to rightful authority without hesitation or resistance

COURTESY: Treating other people with respect, recognizing that all are made in God's image and likeness

---

WAYS OF TURNING AWAY FROM HAPPINESS

MURDER: Have I taken the life of another or been involved in taking the life of another (including abortion)?

THEFT OR ROBBERY: Have I taken what belongs to another, either in secret or publicly?

RESTITUTION: Have I returned to others what I have borrowed or taken from them?

GOSSIP/CALUMNY: Have I disparaged someone's character? Have I accused someone wrongly? Have I caused emotional harm to another by word or deed (e.g. backbiting, gossiping, cursing, or cheating another)?

GOSSIP/DETRACTION: Have I harmed another's good reputation by revealing a truth which should not be told?

SUPERSTITION/THE OCCULT: Have I indulged in superstitious practices or have I used sacred objects in a superstitious way? Have I indulged in horoscopes, tarot cards, Ouija boards, etc.?

DEFAMATION: Have I publicly damaged the character of another through social media?

BODILY MUTILATION: Have I intentionally harmed my body through excessive piercings, tattoos, cutting, starvation, etc.?

IRRELIGION: Have I tried to tempt God's power? Perjured myself under oath? Misused or violated that which is sacred (sacrilege)?

DISOBEDIENCE: Have I willfully disobeyed a command from someone in authority over me? Have I held in contempt that authority or his command?

INGRATITUDE: Have I failed to express thanks for a favor received or failed to notice a favor received?

LYING: Have I intentionally told a falsehood? Have I lied with malicious intent (e.g. to make fun of others, to profit from the lie, etc.)?

DISSIMULATION/HYPOCRISY: Have I acted in such a way to portray myself as someone I am not? Have I behaved in a way that makes me seem like I am better, holier or wiser than I truly am?

COVETOUSNESS: Do I have an inordinate desire for wealth or possessions? Do I desire the goods of others?

PRODIGALITY: Do I spend money needlessly or excessively?

ACTING
WITH PRUDENCE

PRUDENCE: ENABLES ONE TO REASON AND TO ACT RIGHTLY IN ANY GIVEN SITUATION — "RIGHT REASON IN ACTION"

GIFT OF COUNSEL: Enables one to respond fully to direction and guidance from the Lord

CIRCUMSPECTION: Careful consideration of circumstances and consequences

DOCILITY: Willingness to be taught

FORESIGHT: Considering the consequences of one's actions; thinking ahead

WAYS OF TURNING AWAY FROM HAPPINESS

IMPRUDENCE: Have I engaged in risky behavior endangering my soul/well-being or that of others? Have I been thoughtless in my speech or actions?

NEGLIGENCE: Have I neglected my responsibilities as a child of God, spouse, parent or employee?

CARNAL "PRUDENCE": Have I seen carnal/material goods as more important than anything else? Have I been crafty, manipulative or fraudulent in my dealings with others?

Have I utilized integral parts of prudence while making decisions (memory, insight, docility, sagacity (reasonableness), reason, foresight, circumspection, caution)? Have I hastily acted on an impulse or procrastinated through indecisiveness?

CONVERSION

CONTENDING WITH FORTITUDE

FORTITUDE: ENABLES ONE TO ENDURE DIFFICULTIES AND PAIN FOR THE SAKE OF WHAT IS GOOD

GIFT OF FORTITUDE: Moves one to endure difficulties for the sake of eternal life with God

MAGNANIMITY: Seeking with confidence to do great things in God, literally "having a large soul"

PERSEVERANCE: Taking steps necessary to carry out objectives in spite of difficulties

PATIENCE: Bearing present difficulties calmly

WAYS OF TURNING AWAY FROM HAPPINESS

COWARDICE: Do I fail to be virtuous out of inordinate fear?

FOOLHARDINESS: Have I placed myself in danger unnecessarily, out of pride? Do I text message while driving?

PRESUMPTION/VAINGLORY: Have I committed sin presuming God's forgiveness? Have I relied solely on my own capabilities as sufficient to handle anything?

FAINTHEARTEDNESS: Do I take on only what I can handle? Do I refuse to do what I can in a difficult situation, even though it is something I could well handle/overcome?

MEANNESS/LITTLENESS: Do I aspire to do only little things when greater things should be attempted?

NOTES:

_____
_____
_____
_____
_____
_____
_____

MASTERING WITH TEMPERANCE

TEMPERANCE: ENABLES ONE TO BE MODERATE IN THE PLEASURE AND USE OF CREATED GOODS

GIFT OF FEAR OF THE LORD: Brings forth the fear of offending God by sin

MODERATION: Attention to balance in one's life

MODESTY: Purity of heart in action, especially in regards to dress and speech

ORDERLINESS: Keeping oneself physically clean and neat and one's belongings in good order

SELF-CONTROL: Joyful mastery over one's passions and desires

WAYS OF TURNING AWAY FROM HAPPINESS

GLUTTONY: Do I eat or drink excessively? Am I attached to fine foods or drink?

LUST: Have I freely entertained pornographic images on the internet, TV, magazines, etc? Have I entertained impure thoughts?

UNCHASTITY/IMPURITY: Have I abused my own sexuality, e.g., masturbation? Have I acted unchastely with others, e.g., engaged in pre-marital sexual relations or had an affair with someone who is married? Have I been unduly intimate with another person, whether the opposite or the same sex?

ANGER: Has my anger caused me to fight (physically or verbally) with another? Have I sought revenge as a result of a wrong because of inordinate anger?

CURIOSITY: Have I spent time studying things that are sinful/not useful? Do I spend an inordinate amount of time on the internet/texting?

IMMODESTY: Have I been immodest in my dress/behavior/speech?

NOTES:

_____
_____
_____
_____
_____
_____
_____

HOW TO PRAY THE ROSARY

Praying the Rosary or 'the epitome of the whole Gospel' is another means of pondering, with Mary, the life of Christ.

1. Make the Sign of the Cross and pray the Apostles' Creed

I believe in God, the Father Almighty, Creator of heaven and earth; and in Jesus Christ, His only Son, our Lord, Who was conceived by the Holy Spirit, born of the Virgin Mary; suffered under Pontius Pilate, was crucified, died and was buried. He descended into hell; the third day He rose again from the dead; He ascended into heaven, is seated at the right hand of God the Father Almighty; from there He will come to judge the living and the dead. I believe in the Holy Spirit, the Holy Catholic Church, the communion of Saints, the forgiveness of sins, the resurrection of the body, and life everlasting. Amen.

2. Pray the Our Father

Our Father, who art in Heaven, hallowed be Thy name.
Thy Kingdom come, Thy will be done, on earth as it is in heaven.
Give us this day our daily bread, and forgive us our trespasses,
as we forgive those who trespass against us.
And lead us not into temptation, but deliver us from evil. Amen.

3. Pray three Hail Mary's

Hail Mary, full of Grace; the Lord is with thee.
Blessed art thou among women,
and blessed is the fruit of thy womb, Jesus.
Holy Mary, Mother of God,
pray for us sinners,
now and at the hour of our death. Amen.

4. Pray the Glory Be

Glory be to the Father, and to the Son, and to the Holy Spirit; as it was in the beginning, is now, and ever shall be, world without end. Amen.

5. Announce the First Mystery And Pray the Our Father.

6. Pray ten hail Mary's (while meditating on the mystery).

7. Pray the Glory Be.

8. Recite "O my Jesus."

O my Jesus, forgive us our sins, save us from the fire of hell, lead all souls to Heaven, especially those in most need of Thy mercy.

9. Announce the Second Mystery And Pray the Our Father.
(CONTINUE WITH THE 3RD, 4TH, AND 5TH MYSTERIES IN THE SAME WAY)

10. After completing the 5th Mystery, Pray the Salve Regina or Hail Holy Queen.

HAIL HOLY QUEEN

Hail, holy Queen, Mother of Mercy! Our life, our sweetness, and our hope! To thee do we cry, poor banished children of Eve. To thee do we send up our sighs, mourning and weeping in this valley of tears. Turn then, most gracious advocate, thine eyes of mercy toward us, and after this, our exile, show unto us the blessed fruit of thy womb, Jesus. O clement, o loving, o sweet Virgin Mary.

Pray for us, O holy Mother of God, that we may be made worthy of the promises of Christ.

THE MYSTERIES OF THE ROSARY

The Five Joyful Mysteries

1. The Annunciation (Lk. 1:26–38)
2. The Visitation (Lk. 1:40–42)
3. The Nativity (Lk. 2:8–7, Mt. 1)
4. The Presentation (Lk. 2:22–35)
5. The Finding of Jesus in the Temple (Lk. 2:41–52)

The Five Luminous Mysteries

1. The Baptism in the Jordan (Mt. 3:13–17)
2. The Wedding at Cana (Jn. 2:1–2)
3. The Proclamation of the Kingdom (Lk. 7:48–49)
4. The Transfiguration (Mt. 17:1–8)
5. The Institution of the Eucharist (Mt. 26:26–28)

The Five Sorrowful Mysteries

1. The Agony in the Garden (Lk. 22:39–46)
2. The Scourging at the Pillar (Mt. 27:26)
3. The Crowning with Thorns (Mk. 15:20–21)
4. The Carrying of the Cross (Lk. 23:26–32, Jn. 19:16–22)
5. The Crucifixion (Jn. 19:25–30)

The Five Glorious Mysteries

1. The Resurrection (Jn. 20:1–9)
2. The Ascension (Acts 1:9–11)
3. Pentecost (Acts 1:13–14, 2:1–4)
4. The Assumption (Lk. 1:46–49)
5. The Coronation (Rev. 11:19–12:1)

THE LITANY OF THE MOST PRECIOUS BLOOD OF JESUS

Lord, have mercy. — Lord, have mercy
Christ, have mercy. — Christ, have mercy on us.
Lord, have mercy. — Lord, have mercy

Jesus, hear us. — Jesus, graciously hear us.

God, the Father of Heaven, — Have mercy on us.
God, the Son, Redeemer of the world, — Have mercy on us.
God, the Holy Spirit, — Have mercy on us.
Holy Trinity, One God, — Have mercy on us.

Blood of Christ, only–begotten Son of the Eternal Father, — Save us.
Blood of Christ, Incarnate Word of God, — Save us.
Blood of Christ, of the New and Eternal Testament, — Save us.
Blood of Christ, falling upon the earth in the Agony, — Save us.
Blood of Christ, shed profusely in the Scourging, — Save us.
Blood of Christ, flowing forth in the Crowning with Thorns, — Save us.
Blood of Christ, poured out on the Cross, — Save us.
Blood of Christ, price of our salvation, — Save us.
Blood of Christ, without which there is no forgiveness. — Save us.
Blood of Christ, Eucharistic drink and refreshment of souls, — Save us.
Blood of Christ, stream of mercy, — Save us.
Blood of Christ, victor over demons, — Save us.
Blood of Christ, courage of Martyrs, — Save us.
Blood of Christ, strength of Confessors, — Save us.
Blood of Christ, bringing forth Virgins, — Save us.
Blood of Christ, help of those in peril, — Save us.
Blood of Christ, relief of the burdened, — Save us.
Blood of Christ, solace in sorrow, — Save us.
Blood of Christ, hope of the penitent, — Save us.
Blood of Christ, consolation of the dying, — Save us.
Blood of Christ, peace and tenderness of hearts, — Save us.
Blood of Christ, pledge of eternal life, — Save us.
Blood of Christ, freeing souls from purgatory, — Save us.
Blood of Christ, most worthy of all glory and honor, — Save us.

Lamb of God, who take away the sins of the world. — Spare us, O Lord
Lamb of God, who take away the sins of the world, — Graciously hear us, O Lord.
Lamb of God, who take away the sins of the world, — Have mercy on us.

V. You have redeemed us, O Lord, in your Blood.
R. And made us, for our God, a kingdom.

Let us pray: Almighty and eternal God, you have appointed your only–begotten Son the Redeemer of the world, and willed to be appeased by his Blood. Grant we beg of you, that we may worthily adore this price of our salvation, and through its power be safeguarded from the evils of the present life, so that we may rejoice in its fruits forever in heaven. Through the same Christ our Lord. Amen.

ANIMA CHRISTI

Soul of Christ, sanctify me.
Body of Christ, save me.
Blood of Christ, inebriate me.
Water from the side of Christ, wash me.
Passion of Christ, strengthen me.
O Good Jesus, hear me.
Within your wounds hide me.
Permit me not to be separated from you.
From the wicked foe, defend me.
At the hour of my death, call me
And bid me come to you,
That with your saints
I may praise you forever and ever. Amen.

TO GOD THE HOLY SPIRIT

Come, O Spirit of Fortitude, and give fortitude to our souls. Make our hearts strong in all trials and in all distress, pouring forth abundantly into them the gifts of strength, that we may be able to resist the attacks of the devil.

Come, Holy Spirit! Drive far away from us our foes from hell, and grant us Your peace. Through all perils guide us safely. Amen.

MEMORARE TO OUR LADY

REMEMBER, O most gracious Virgin Mary, that never was it known that anyone who fled to thy protection, implored thy help, or sought thy intercession was left unaided. Inspired with this confidence, I fly to thee, O Virgin of virgins, my Mother; to thee do I come; before thee I stand, sinful and sorrowful. O Mother of the Word Incarnate, despise not my petitions, but in thy mercy hear and answer me. Amen.

CHAPLET OF DIVINE MERCY

1. Make the Sign of the Cross and pray one Our Father

Our Father, who art in Heaven, hallowed be Thy name.
Thy Kingdom come, Thy will be done, on earth as it is in heaven. Give us this day our daily bread, and forgive us our trespasses, as we forgive those who trespass against us. And lead us not into temptation, but deliver us from evil. Amen.

2. Pray one Hail Mary

Hail Mary, full of Grace; the Lord is with thee. Blessed art thou among women, and blessed is the fruit of thy womb, Jesus.
Holy Mary, Mother of God, pray for us sinners, now and at the hour of our death. Amen.

3. Pray the Apostles' Creed

Jesus I Trust in You!

I believe in God, the Father Almighty,
Creator of heaven and earth;
and in Jesus Christ, His only Son, our Lord,
Who was conceived by the Holy Spirit,
born of the Virgin Mary;
suffered under Pontius Pilate,
was crucified, died and was buried.
He descended into hell;
the third day He rose again from the dead;
He ascended into heaven,
is seated at the right hand of God the Father Almighty;
from there He will come to judge the living and the dead.
I believe in the Holy Spirit, the Holy Catholic Church,
the communion of Saints, the forgiveness of sins, the resurrection of the body, and life everlasting. Amen.

4. To start each decade, pray the Eternal Father

Eternal Father, I offer you the Body and Blood, Soul and Divinity, of your dearly Beloved Son, our Lord, Jesus Christ, in atonement for our sins, and those of the whole world.

5. On the ten small beads, pray:

For the sake of His sorrowful Passion, have mercy on us, and on the whole world.

6. Repeat steps four and five for each decade. After completing the fifth decade, pray three times:

Holy God, Holy Mighty One, Holy Immortal One, have mercy on us, and on the whole world.

RENEWAL OF BAPTISMAL PROMISES

O Lord, my God, this day I renew my baptismal vows: I renounce sin, so that I can live in freedom as a child of God. I renounce the snares of the devil, so that sin cannot enslave me. I renounce Satan and all his works and all his pomps. I take Jesus Christ for my Deliverer and my Champion, my Model and my Guide. I promise to serve Him faithfully, whatever the cost, to the end of my life so that I can share in His everlasting triumph. Amen

ST. FRANCIS PRAYER BEFORE THE CRUCIFIX

O Most High and glorious God, enlighten the darkness of my heart. Give me, Lord, a firm faith, sure hope, and perfect love, profound humility—the sign and knowledge so that I may carry out all Your commandments. Amen.

O crux, ave, spes unica.
Hail, O Cross, our only hope!

PRAYER TO SAINT MICHAEL

Saint Michael the Archangel, defend us in battle, be our protection against the malice and snares of the devil. May God rebuke him we humbly pray; and do thou, O Prince of the Heavenly host, by the power of God, thrust into hell Satan and all evil spirits who wander through the world for the ruin of souls. Amen.

IN BAPTISM WE ARE GRAFTED ONTO CHRIST THE VINE;

He enters us and remains in us as long as we desire His presence. By freely choosing to live as one with Christ, we permit Him to transform us from within. This life in Christ is rooted in the virtues and gifts received at Baptism (*CCC* 1266).

If faith is like the root, charity is like the sap that nourishes the trunk and rises into the branches, the network of virtues, to produce the delicious fruit of good works." (Servais Pinckaers, O.P., Morality: The Catholic View, South Bend, St. Augustine Press, 2001)

The Disciple of Christ Virtues will guide you in identifying virtues which need to be cultivated. Each corresponding "Opposing Trait" highlights a pattern of behavior which needs change in order for you to mature in virtue.

Human virtues acquired by education, by deliberate acts, and by perseverance ever-renewed in repeated efforts are purified and elevated by divine grace. With God's help, they forge character and give facility in the practice of the good. The virtuous man is happy to practice them (*CCC*, 1810).

"GOD CAUSES THE GROWTH"
(1 COR. 3:7)

DISCIPLE OF CHRIST VIRTUES

IN BAPTISM WE ARE GRAFTED ONTO CHRIST THE VINE; He enters us and remains in us as long as we desire His presence. By freely choosing to live as one with Christ, we permit Him to transform us from within. This life in Christ is rooted in the virtues and gifts received at baptism (see *CCC*, 1266).

"If faith is like the root, charity is like the sap that nourishes the trunk and rises into the branches, the network of virtues, to produce the delicious fruit of good works" (Servais Pinckaers, O.P., *Morality: The Catholic View*, South Bend, St. Augustine Press, 2001).

Disciple of Christ Virtues guide educators, parents, and students in identifying virtues which need to be cultivated. Each corresponding "Opposing Trait" highlights a pattern of behavior which needs change in order for one to mature in virtue.

Human virtues acquired by education, by deliberate acts, and by perseverance ever-renewed in repeated efforts are purified and elevated by divine grace. With God's help, they forge character and give facility in the practice of the good. The virtuous man is happy to practice them (CCC, 1810).

"GOD GIVES THE GROWTH."
(1 CORINTHIANS 3:7)

VIRTUE	MEANING	OPPOSING TRAIT	WAYS TO CULTIVATE
JUSTICE (Fairness)	Enables one to give to each, beginning with God, what is due him	Failing to see what is owed to each by virtue of his dignity	Recognize what is due to God first and then to others.
AFFABILITY	Being easy to approach and easy to talk to — friendly	Being mean, unkind, cruel, or unflattering	Smile; acknowledge the presence of other people and take time to listen to them.
COURTESY	Treating other people with respect, recognizing that all are made in God's image and likeness	Not recognizing the inherent dignity of others made in God's image and likeness	Be aware of others' feelings and expressions; be polite, well-mannered.
GENEROSITY	Giving of oneself in a willing and cheerful manner for the good of others	Giving without a spirit of cheer, with a begrudging manner	Be self-giving; focus on one act of charity/kindness each day; share.
GRATITUDE	Thankful disposition of mind and heart	Not expressing appreciation; taking other people and things for granted	Count the good things (blessings) in one's life; express gratitude even when it is difficult.
KINDNESS	Expressing genuine concern about the well-being of others; anticipating their needs	Not regarding the well-being of others, being cruel in looks, words, and actions	Practice speaking, thinking, and acting kindly.
LOYALTY	Accepting the bonds implicit in relationships and defending the virtues upheld by Church, family, and country	Breaking bonds of trust with Church, family, country, friends, and school	Seek to do one's best to help others; follow rules; fulfill responsibilities; be faithful to commitments.
OBEDIENCE	Assenting to rightful authority without hesitation or resistance	Resisting the directives of rightful authority	Listen to rightful authority; follow directions; give a prompt response.
PATRIOTISM	Paying due honor and respect to one's country, with a willingness to serve	Lacking regard or respect for one's country and national symbols	Show respect for your country's flag; speak respectfully about government officials; recite the Pledge.
PRAYERFULNESS	Being still, listening, and being willing to talk to God as a friend	Entertaining distractions during prayers and Mass	Cultivate a spirit of prayer and recollection; maintain the proper posture (kneeling, sitting still, etc.).
RESPECT	Speaking and acting according to one's own and others' rights, status, and circumstances	Resisting the directives of rightful authority	Be respectful in words and actions (body language); allow others to go first.
RESPONSIBILITY	Fulfilling one's just duties; accepting the consequences of one's words and actions, intentional and unintentional	Failing to accept responsibility for one's words and/or actions; being unreliable	Be accountable for one's personal actions and decisions at home, at school, and in personal relationships.
SINCERITY	Trustfulness in words and actions; honesty and enthusiasm towards others	Speaking or acting in a manner only to make oneself look good; being insincere	Tell the whole truth; build trust by words and actions; state what one is sorry for.
TRUSTWORTHINESS	Acting in a way that inspires confidence and trust; being reliable	Being devious or deceptive	Perform actions that restore and maintain trust; act with fidelity in small matters.

VIRTUE	MEANING	OPPOSING TRAIT	WAYS TO CULTIVATE
PRUDENCE (Sound Judgment)	Enables one to reason and to act rightly in any given situation — "right reason in action"	Being hasty or rash in one's words or actions	Pray for guidance. Seek sound advice. Think about the situation. Act upon the decision.
PARTS OF A PRUDENTIAL ACT			
GOOD COUNSEL (Ask and listen)	Seeking advice from a reasonable person	Seeking advice from those who agree with you; asking moral advice from people who do not share your moral values	Seek advice from trustworthy people.
GOOD JUDGMENT (Think)	Thinking rightly about a decision	Acting without thinking	Carefully consider all the circumstances and ask "What am I to do now?"
COMMAND (Act)	Directly acting upon a sound decision	Failing to act upon a sound decision	Take action after thoughtful deliberation.
VIRTUES			
CIRCUMSPECTION	Careful consideration of circumstances and consequences	Considering only oneself when acting	Seek advice silently reflect upon the circumstances and consequences of one's actions (memory).
DOCILITY	Willingness to be taught	Being stubborn, inflexible, and proudly set in one's ways	Listen to others and be willing to follow directions; thank others for rightful corrections.
FORESIGHT	Consideration of the consequences of one's actions; thinking ahead	Failing to consider later consequences	Pray, think, act; learn how to gather information to make a decision; plan out long-term and short-term goals.

VIRTUE	MEANING	OPPOSING TRAIT	WAYS TO CULTIVATE
FORTITUDE (Courage)	Enables one to endure difficulties and pain for the sake of what is good	Choosing the easiest task; being cowardly; being insensible to fear	Withstand difficulties; complete hard tasks.
INDUSTRIOUSNESS	Diligence, especially in work that leads to natural and supernatural maturity	Giving in to a lack of motivation to complete one's responsibilities; being lazy	Diligently complete a task; set small goals along the way.
MAGNANIMITY	Seeking with confidence to do great things in God; literally "having a large soul"	Seeking to do great things for self-promotion — not seeking to do the good that is possible — pusillanimity (weak, spineless)	Acknowledge the good in others when it is difficult; strive to do difficult tasks with God's grace.
MAGNIFICENCE	Doing great things for God	Being wasteful; not responding to grace	Use one's talents for the good; act with generosity towards others.
PATIENCE	Bearing present difficulties calmly	Being impatient while completing a difficult task or in handling challenging circumstances	Listen to others; wait for one's turn; tolerate inconveniences and annoyances without complaining.
PERSEVERANCE	Taking the steps necessary to carry out objectives in spite of difficulties	Quickly giving up when a task is challenging	Complete task from start to finish; stay with a task when it is hard, difficult, or boring.

VIRTUE	MEANING	OPPOSING TRAIT	WAYS TO CULTIVATE
TEMPERANCE (Self-Control)	Enables one to be moderate in the pleasure and use of created goods	Intemperance; overindulging in a good thing	Exercise the freedom to say "no" to one's wants and desires.
HONESTY	Sincerity, openness and truthfulness in one's words and actions	Being dishonest in words and actions; telling lies	Live uprightly in words and actions; recognize that "God sees the heart."
HUMILITY	Awareness that all one's gifts come from God and appreciation for the gifts of others	Failing to recognize the gifts of others; being too proud or having false humility	Show deference to others; acknowledge the accomplishments of others; look at one's strengths and weaknesses honestly.
MEEKNESS	Serenity of spirit while focusing on the needs of others	Giving in to anger and losing one's temper when working or playing with others	Remain calm; allow others to go first; wait without complaining.
MODERATION	Attention to balance in one's life	Giving in to being excessive in one or more areas of one's life	Set limits for oneself; create a balance in one's life by limiting the use of media, consumption of additional food and drink, etc.
MODESTY	Purity of heart in action, especially in regards to dress and speech	Choosing to dress or act in a way inconsistent with one's dignity as a child of God	Follow the dress code; recognize your dignity as a person; ask yourself if you are respecting yourself as a child of God.
ORDERLINESS	Keeping oneself physically clean and neat and one's belongings in good order	Disorder with regard to one's space and physical appearance	Establish order in one's daily life; keep one's space and appearance orderly and clean.
SELF-CONTROL	Joyful mastery over one's passions and desires	Being excessive in words or actions, acting impulsively	Mastery of one's desires; practice restraint in regard to words and actions.

CORPORAL WORKS OF MERCY

† **GIVE FOOD TO THE HUNGRY:** Making a personal sacrifice to nourish another person's body and soul

† **GIVE DRINK TO THE THIRSTY:** Giving others refreshment to sustain their physical and spiritual life

† **CLOTHE THE NAKED:** Aiding others in recognizing the dignity of their bodies by treating them in a manner that expresses this dignity

† **SHELTER THE HOMELESS:** Welcoming others and making them feel at home; giving them an experience of kindness and security

† **VISIT THE SICK:** Supporting those bearing Christ's Cross with your prayer and presence

† **VISIT THE IMPRISONED:** Reaching out through prayer and kind support to those in prison or who have less freedom

† **BURY THE DEAD:** Laying to rest the body of someone who has died and helping their loved ones grieve

SPIRITUAL WORKS OF MERCY

† **TEACHING THE IGNORANT:** Teaching others the knowledge they need to be happy and fulfilled in this life and in the next

† **COUNSEL THE DOUBTFUL:** Bringing peace of mind to another through good advice and uplifting words and deeds

† **ADMONISH THE SINNER:** Calling others to conversion and encouraging them in pursuit of holiness

† **BEAR WRONGS PATIENTLY:** Receiving slights, insults, and inconveniences cheerfully and without judging or expressing irritation

† **FORGIVE OFFENSES:** Extending God's merciful love to someone who has hurt you, and letting go of his or her guilt

† **COMFORT THE SORROWFUL:** Lightening another's burden of sorrow through care and compassion

† **PRAY FOR THE LIVING & THE DEAD:** Loving your neighbor as yourself through interceding for the needs of all

"What good is it, my brothers, if someone says he has faith but does not have works? Can that faith save him? If a brother or sister has nothing to wear and has no food for the day, and one of you says to them, "Go in peace, keep warm, and eat well," but you do not give them the necessities of the body, what good is it? So also faith of itself, if it does not have works, is dead." —James 2:14–17

"God is love" (1 John 4:8), and so everything that He does is rooted in the foundation of His love. Your existence is rooted in His love. To be a disciple of Christ means to live, ever more deeply, in the mystery of God's love for you personally. His love is the foundation of your life, of your identity, of your being. His love is what is my sure support, "my refuge, my fortress, my God in whom I trust" (Psalm 91:1).

When His love is the foundation of your identity and worth, you are free to love Him in return. To be a disciple of Christ means to love God above all things and your neighbor as yourself. Practicing the works of mercy is a concrete way to show your love of God and neighbor.

NOTES:

_____

_____

_____

_____

_____

_____

_____

_____

_____

_____

Cover/Sunday Artwork: *Scenes from the Passion of Christ*, Hans Memling, ca. 1470, Galleria Sabauda, Turin / Public Domain

Page 4: *The Last Supper* (tempera on panel), Gaddi, Taddeo (c.1300–66) / Galleria dell' Accademia & Museo degli Strumenti Musicali, Florence, Tuscany, Italy / Bridgeman Images

Page 7: *The Last Judgment*, Fra Angelico, 1431 / Wikipedia / Public Domain

Page 9: *The Adoration of the Child with St. John the Baptist and St. Romauld of Ravenna* \ c.1463 Lippi, Fra Filippo (c.1406–69) / Galleria degli Uffizi, Florence, Italy / Bridgeman Images

Page 11: Wikipedia / Public Domain

Page 15: *Detail of The Feast in the House of Levi*, 1573 (detail of 227605), Veronese, (Paolo Caliari) (1528–88) / Gallerie dell'Accademia, Venice, Italy / Bridgeman Images

Page 25: *Secret between Brothers,* Durand (Contemporary Artist) / www.durand–gallery.com / Bridgeman Images

Page 35: *St. Lazarus and the Rich Epulon,* (oil on canvas) / Mondadori Portfolio/ Electa/Paolo Manusardi / Bridgeman Images

Page 37: *The Corner Stone*, illustration from 'The Life of Our Lord Jesus Christ', 1886–94), Tissot, James Jacques Joseph (1836–1902) / Brooklyn Museum of Art, New York, USA / Purchased by Public Subscription / Bridgeman Images

Page 39: *Return of the Prodigal Son*, (oil on canvas), Licinio, Bernardino (c.1489-c.1560) / National Museum of Art of Romania, Bucharest, Romania / Cameraphoto Arte Venezia / Bridgeman Images

Page 43: *Christ Escapes the Pharisees* (oil on canvas), Overbeck, Friedrich (1789–1869) / Koninklijk Museum voor Schone Kunsten, Antwerp, Belgium / © Lukas – Art in Flanders VZW / Bridgeman Images

Page 48: *Archangel Michael Fights Satan*, c.1590 (oil on canvas), Tintoretto, Jacopo Robusti (1518-94) / Gemaeldegalerie Alte Meister, Dresden, Germany / © Staatliche Kunstsammlungen Dresden / Bridgeman Images

Page 50: *Adoration of the Shepherds with the Father God in a Glory of Angels*, by Anton Raphael Mengs, 1728–1779, / De Agostini Picture Library / A. Dagli Orti / Bridgeman Images

Page 55: *Jesus and the Centurion* (oil on canvas), Veronese, (Paolo Caliari) (1528–88) / Prado, Madrid, Spain / Public Domain

Page 63: *Nicodemus*, Copping, Harold (1863–1932) / Private Collection / Bridgeman Images

Page 67: *Christ and the Adulteress,* Jacopo Tintoretto, 1555, Wikimedia Commons / Public Domain

Page 69: *Jesus Found in the Temple*, illustration for 'The Life of Christ', c.1886–94, Tissot, James Jacques Joseph (1836–1902) / Brooklyn Museum of Art, New York, USA / Bridgeman Images

Page 71: *View of the apse depicting the Christ Pantocrator and the Virgin at Prayer Surrounded by Archangels*, 1148 (mosaic)), Byzantine School, (12th century) / Duomo, Cefalu, Sicily, Italy/ Bridgeman Images

Page 73: *Disputa*, from the Stanza della Segnatura, 1508–11 (fresco), Raphael (Raffaello Sanzio of Urno) / Vatican Museums and Galleries, Vatican City / Bridgman Images

CREDITS

Page 75: *The Jews Took up Rocks to Stone Him,* illustration for 'The Life of Christ' c.1886-96, Tissot, James Jacques Joseph (1836-1902) / Brooklyn Museum of Art, New York, USA / Bridgeman Images

Page 82: *The Last Supper,* Domenico Ghirlandaio, 1486 (Fresco) / San Marco, Italy / © Linda Kelly 2017

Page 83: *Saint Peter Repentant* by anonymous artist of Bologna, 1600–1610, Italian School, (17th century) / Pinacoteca Ambrosiana, Milan, Italy / De Agostini Picture Library/ Bridgeman Images

Judas Repents and Returns the Money, Illustration for 'The Life of Christ', c.1886–94, Tissot, James Jacques Joseph (1836–1902) / Brooklyn Museum of Art, New York, USA / Bridgeman Images

Page 85: *Judas Goes to the Find the Jews,* illustration from 'The Life of Our Lord Jesus Christ', 1886–94 (w/c over graphite on paper), Tissot, James Jacques Joseph (1836–1902) / Brooklyn Museum of Art, New York, USA / Bridgeman Images

Page 87: *Christ Washing the Disciples' Feet,* c.1305 (fresco) (post restoration), Giotto di Bondone (c.1266-1337) / Scrovegni (Arena) Chapel, Padua, Italy / Alinari / Bridgman Images

Pages 92–98: *Illustration for The Life of Christ,* Stations of the Cross, Tissot, James Jacques Joseph / Brooklyn Museum of Art, New York, USA / Bridgeman Images

Page 100: *The Descent into Limbo,* 1442 (fresco), Angelico, Fra (Guido di Pietro) / Museo di San Marco dell'Angelico, Florence, Italy / Wikipedia / Public Domain

Page 101: *Resurrection of Christ and the Pious Women at the Sepulchre,* 1442 (fresco), Angelico, Fra (Guido di Pietro) (c.1387–1455) / Museo di San Marco dell'Angelico, Florence, Italy / Wikimedia Commons / Public Domain

Page 103: *The Dream of St. Joseph,* c.1700, Giordano, Luca (1634–1705) / Indianapolis Museum of Art at Newfields, USA / Martha Delzell Memorial Fund / Bridgeman Images

Page 105: *Annunciation,* 1501 (fresco), Pinturicchio, Bernardino di Betto (c.1452–1513) / Baglioni Chapel, Santa Maria Maggiore, Spello, Italy / Bridgeman Images

Page 113: *Mother Teresa* (1910-1997) peace Nobel prize in 1979, here in Calcutta with underpriviledged child, in the 80's / Bridgeman Images

Public Domain, Wikimedia Commons

Page 114: *Return of the Prodigal Son* (c. 1667–1670) by Bartolomé Esteban Murillo oil on canvas / National Gallery of Art, Washington / Wikimedia Commons / Public Domain

St. Maximilian Kolbe / Wikimedia Commons / Artist Unknown / Public Domain

Page 121: *The Rich Young Man Went Away Sorrowful, illustration from 'The Life of Our Lord Jesus Christ',* 1886-96 (w/c over graphite on paper), Tissot, James Jacques Joseph (1836-1902) / Brooklyn Museum of Art, New York, USA / Purchased by Public Subscription / Bridgeman Images

Page 126: The Crucifixion (fresco), Giotto di Bondone (c.1266–1337) / San Francesco, Lower Church, Assisi, Italy / Alinari / Bridgeman Images

Page 129: *Saint Michael banishes the devil to the abyss,* 1665/68, Murillo, Bartolome Esteban (1618–82) / Kunsthistorisches Museum, Vienna, Austria / Bridgeman Images